UNIFORM WITH THIS BOOK

THE
ROMNEY, HYTHE &
DYMCHURCH RAILWAY

by

W. J. K. DAVIES

DAVID & CHARLES: NEWTON ABBOT LONDON
NORTH POMFRET (VT) VANCOUVER

ISBN 0 7153 6827 3

Set in 10 on 12pt Linotype Plantin and printed in
Great Britain by Latimer Trend & Company Ltd Plymouth
for David & Charles (Holdings) Limited
South Devon House Newton Abbot Devon

Published in the United States of America
by David & Charles Inc
North Pomfret Vermont 05053 USA

Published in Canada
by Douglas David & Charles Limited
132 Philip Avenue North Vancouver BC

To the memory of
The late Captain J. E. P. Howey
and
The late Henry Greenly
without whom there would have
been no RH & DR, this book
is dedicated.

Contents

List of Illustrations

PLATES

LINE DRAWINGS IN TEXT

Foreword

It gives me great pleasure to be asked to write a foreword to this official history of the Romney, Hythe and Dymchurch Railway.

For twenty-seven years I have worked on the railway, usually engine-driving in the season and engaged in maintenance in the off-season and, for most of that time, I have been responsible for the day-to-day operation of the line. To my everlasting regret, I never met Henry Greenly, the man responsible for the design of the railway and its equipment, but for 17 years I had almost daily contact with Captain John Howey and it was he, of course, who financed the project and owned the railway until his death in 1963.

In this book Keith Davies tells the story of the collaboration of these two men and the truly remarkable little railway which was the result, from the earliest days until the present day, a far from easy task considering the paucity of records and the often conflicting nature of a large proportion of the small amount of evidence that is available. I know something of the amount of research undertaken by Mr Davies and the trouble involved in verifying many of his facts and I am sure that the book is as accurate a history as it is possible to produce at this time.

Those of us who love the Romney Railway can consider ourselves fortunate in having in the author a man able and prepared to spend so much of his time on the production of this book and one who possesses the necessary literary ability and 'feel' for his subject. I warmly commend this story of the most ambitious miniature railway experiment ever—a truly living memorial to the genius of Greenly and the determination and enthusiasm of Howey—a railway that almost half a century after opening still retains its unique position among the railways of the world.   GEORGE BARLOW

CHAPTER 1

Prologue

In the beginning—if one may say so without irreverence—was Heywood, and Sir Arthur Heywood both initiated studies of the 15in gauge as a practical one and laid down dogma as to its use. Sir Arthur Percival Heywood, Bart, of Duffield Bank in Derbyshire, to give him his full title, was a wealthy Victorian who was intensely interested in engineering. In particular he was concerned to provide cheap effective transport for large estates and he came to the conclusion that a railway with the gauge of 15in was probably the smallest on which full size practice could be used. His dicta are well known: the line should be built to the maximum loading gauge; the suspension should be by rubber blocks instead of springs; locomotives should have equal overhang fore and aft and all wheels should be coupled to provide maximum adhesion. Some stood the test of time and others did not: perhaps his most famous, that cabs were unnecessary and that 'a stout macintosh is both cheaper and better for the driver' produced the most lurid comments in after years. Good or bad, from 1874 on, Sir Arthur devoted much of his time to promoting his ideas and trying them out in practice on his own estate. Regrettably they did not attain much popularity but he did build one railway whose existence is directly relevant to this history. In 1895 the Duke of Westminster engaged him to build an estate railway from Balderton Station on the Great Western Railway to the Duke's mansion at Eaton Hall. The three-mile line became one of the show pieces of small railways and was used for trials by two of the major personalities connected with the subject of this book.

ENTER GREENLY AND HOWEY

These were Henry Greenly and Mr (later Captain) J. E. P. Howey. Ironically their interest in the line was far removed from Heywood's original ideas for both were interested in miniature (scale model) railways rather than in very narrow gauge ones. Henry Greenly was first and foremost a model engineer and his design inspirations came from contemporary American practice. Born in 1875, he served an engineering apprenticeship with the Metropolitan Railway and also studied architecture before joining the editorial staff of the *Model Engineer*. There—and later—he was involved with the design of small-scale models up to two- or three-inch gauge and his articles attracted the attention of another colourful character of the period, W. J. Bassett-Lowke. Bassett-Lowke had an interest in a light engineering business and he used Greenly first as a consulting engineer, and then as a partner in a new firm Miniature Railways of Great Britain Ltd. This firm was set up in 1904 to build and run 15in gauge amusement railways and the gauge chosen was almost certainly not selected because of Heywood. The American Cagney brothers had been using it for scale model passenger carrying lines for some years and had indirectly provided locomotives for a private railway at Blakesley Hall near Towcester, Northants. Both Bassett-Lowke and Greenly knew this line and by all accounts were greatly influenced by it. They both believed in the 'scale model' idea and Greenly's first 15in gauge design for the company was an elegant, quarter-scale 4-4-2—the almost legendary *Little Giant*. As engineer to the firm he developed this design over the following ten years, becoming involved too in the design of other railway features. His work in this field culminated in the design of Rhyl Miniature Railway in 1911, for which he designed every thing from route to buildings, rolling stock to locomotive. He produced 'total' designs similarly for the company's successor Narrow Gauge Railways Ltd, whose main early efforts were devoted to building exhibition lines on the continent.

At about this point, Mr J. E. P. Howey enters the picture. Young and wealthy, he was by the 1910s already very intrigued by small railways and had shown considerable interest in the work of both Bassett-Lowke and Greenly. On moving to Staughton Manor, a country house he rented in 1912, he was able to develop a 9½in gauge garden railway, formerly at his Woodbridge home. At Staughton it ran through the grounds of the house and its adjoining farm. It was powered by a true-scale Great Northern-type Atlantic designed by Henry Greenly and built by Bassett-Lowke and had such model features as a scale station and a miniature Forth Bridge designed by the ubiquitous Greenly. An amusing photograph of the period shows Howey, Greenly and one other demonstrating the principle of the cantilever with Howey's dog Peter slung in a bag to represent the balance weight; it may be said in passing that Howey's dogs must have been among the most travelled railway-pets anywhere. They seem to have accompanied him everywhere and were often photographed riding in the tender both at Staughton and on the Romney, Hythe & Dymchurch. A later one even braved the 'Romney's' open scooter on occasion and at least once suffered a sore head from being shot off when the scooter came to an abrupt stop as it hit some trucks.

HOWEY'S AMBITIONS

Mr Howey, as he then was, was not satisfied for long with his 9½in gauge line. He wanted a 'real' railway and in the autumn of 1913 commissioned Bassett-Lowke to produce him a 15in gauge locomotive bigger and more powerful than any that had gone before. Henry Greenly accordingly designed the ultimate extension of the *Little Giant*, a 4-6-2 or Pacific locomotive that was basically a stretched class 30 *Little Giant* with a longer boiler and with another pair of coupled wheels inserted. As one of the only two Pacific-type locomotives in Great Britain at the time (the other was the GWR's *Great Bear*) it excited much attention from the railway press; it also produced a fair amount of confusion since Bassett-Lowke's after branding the type *Colossus* decided to rename the class *Gigantic* and doctored photographs of the locomotive at Staughton Manor to show this name. Howey himself named it *John Anthony* after his son and in July 1914 took the locomotive to Eaton Hall to see just what it could do. The war broke out in August of that year and *John Anthony* stayed in Balderton shed while Lt Howey went to war, became Captain Howey . . . and was taken prisoner on 11 November 1916. While Howey languished in a German prisoner-of-war camp, Henry Greenly was employed on Government work and they apparently did not meet again until the early 1920s. By that time Greenly was consulting engineer to the Ravenglass & Eskdale Railway and was developing his idea that a 15in gauge locomotive should be over scale if it was to be really effective. He first tried out this idea with some 4–4–2s designed for Rhyl before 1914 and built in 1919-20, and in the 1920s developed it further with the massive one-third scale 2–8–2 *River Esk* for the Ravenglass & Eskdale. Meanwhile Captain Howey had returned to England railwayless, (the Staughton line having been sold) but still fascinated by the 15in gauge and itching to build a railway on which he could drive fast. Furthermore he formed a friendship with another famous racing driver of the period, Count Louis Zborowski of Chitty-Chitty Bang-Bang fame, and the count was also fascinated by the miniature railway idea. Since Henry Greenly was by now (1924) the pre-eminent designer of miniature lines, at least in Great Britain, it was inevitable that the three would get together. That a serious railway rather than a garden line was envisaged by all of them is obvious from the commission given jointly to Greenly late in 1924 to design a one-third scale express locomotive. No doubt all had visions of somewhere with good stretches of straight track but surely no one at the time would have envisaged that the final project—realised only after one of them had died—would bring together elements of the work not only of Heywood and Greenly but also of the other eminent designer of 15in gauge railways in Europe at that time. This was Greenly's German acquaintance, Roland Martens who was designer of light locomotives for the firm of Krauss & Co, Munich. From various sources, it is obvious that the two men freely exchanged ideas and possibly even helped each other directly. Certainly Martens was responsible in his own right for some very fine 15in gauge Pacifics and in some ways his designs were in advance of Greenly's. Yet in the last event he was purely a locomotive designer. Henry Greenly's versatility made him a *railway* designer and it was that versatility which led directly to the Romney, Hythe & Dymchurch Railway as we know it today.

Page 17 (above) *The Masterminds at work ... Captain Howey (standing) and Henry Greenly (bending) 'survey' the site of New Romney station; (below) And waiting ... for the Duke of York in August 1926. Greenly is leaning over the locomotive while Howey, appearing slightly blasé about the whole thing, is in the tender*

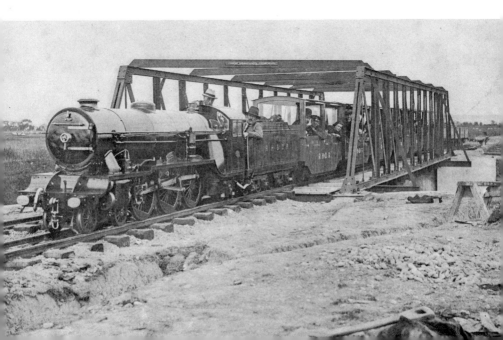

Page 18 Nos 3, 5, 7 and 8 under construction at Davey Paxman's Works. In the original print the name Southern Chief can be clearly seen on the front locomotive

CHAPTER 2

Inception of the Railway

For a railway built so recently, the events surrounding the inception of the Romney, Hythe & Dymchurch railway are very obscure. Its promoters—a mixture of enthusiastic amateurs in the best sense of the word and of professional engineers—were not overkeen on keeping records anyway and were in any case conflicting and slightly eccentric in their personalities. In consequence, a number of varying stories were spread around, both then and later, while the physical plant underwent a series of rapid and drastic changes that would have shaken a conventional railway to the core; since the 'Romney' was effectively the private plaything of one man, and regarded by the district as a 'toy', they passed largely unnoticed.

PRELIMINARIES

For years the conventional 'legend' of the RH & D's birth was that fostered consciously or unconsciously by Captain Howey in his later years. This was to the effect that he and his equally famous rival and friend Count Zborowski had made a pact, in 1924, to give up motor racing and start a 'real' 15in gauge railway together. The railway was to be between New Romney and Hythe, this having been suggested by Sir Herbert Walker, then general manager of the Southern Railway; each man accordingly ordered a locomotive to Henry Greenly's latest design and went off to his last race. Unfortunately, Zborowski's car crashed and he was killed. A sorrowing Howey, or so the story went, was left to perpetuate his friend's memory by taking over Zborowski's locomotive and building the railway they had planned. Unfortunately this tale appears to be rather romanticised (and inaccurate) recollection. There is plenty of documentary evidence that the RH & D as such was *not* in prospect at

19

the time of Zborowski's death and although the design was commissioned by both men, *both* original Pacifics (later RH & D 1 and 2) were ordered by Count Zborowski, apparently for the 15in gauge line he was building at Higham, near Canterbury. He was very interested in this and had already acquired a Bassett-Lowke Class 30 Atlantic as a stop-gap at short notice. There was presumably a strong link between the two men and it is probable that they had discussed the idea of a long 15in gauge line since after Zborowski's death Captain Howey took over both Pacifics then under construction; in evidence at the RH & D public inquiry it was stated that he had them as a legacy from the dead man. It would appear, however, that it was only early in 1925 that Captain Howey started looking round for a site to build a public railway to run them on. His ideas were probably stimulated by the already existing Ravenglass & Eskdale Railway which had just been acquired by Sir Aubrey Brocklebank, chairman of the Cunard Shipping Line and a local Eskdale resident. Howey clearly was still looking for a site since he offered to buy the R & ER with the intention of extending it to Ambleside; it was only after his offer was rejected that he started looking for somewhere else.

THE SITE AGREED

It is likely that in his search he was influenced by the ideas of Henry Greenly, who had been deeply involved with the Eskdale line and had designed Zborowski's Pacifics. Both Howey and Greenly later claimed that Sir Herbert Walker, of the Southern Railway, had suggested the idea of the Romney Marsh area to them; Greenly, at various public meetings in 1925, indeed said that it was he who had persuaded Captain Howey to develop the line there. Whatever may be the exact truth—and memories are often deceptive—the coast site between Hythe and the twin towns of New Romney and Littlestone was certainly almost ideal. It lay between the termini of two Southern Railway branches and the Southern, although being pressed to do so, did not much want to extend either; it encompassed a number of rapidly developing holiday camps which would provide the summer holiday traffic essential to such a line as Howey and Greenly envisaged; it was reasonably flat so that no major engineering works would be needed and the 'run' would suit the large-wheeled Pacifics. Once this site had been agreed, and the consent of the Southern Railway secured, work on the project started in earnest in August 1925. It was prefaced by a visit to Ravenglass where the first Pacific, now named *Green Goddess,* after a favourite play of Captain Howey's, was tried out under field conditions.* In spite of the different nature of that line, she performed all that was expected of her and a film taken at the time was later used to great effect at residents' meetings on Romney Marsh.

WORK BEGINS

The whole start of the RH & D shows evidence of a surprising confidence and hustle. Since its course involved acquiring land and crossing public roads, it was plain that a light railway order would be needed. Obviously all concerned thought that this would be little more than a formality since by September 1925 all the vital personnel were installed in hotels at New Romney or Littlestone, the two completed Pacifics were stored in Binns' garage at Littlestone and Captain Howey's future home 'Red Tiles' was already being planned. At this time, of course, the company had not yet been formed and all correspondence, etc, was being carried out by Henry Greenly who had entered the scheme as Captain Howey's agent, with the intention that he should both design the railway and then become its manager and engineer. Captain Howey, as the promoter, was to put up most of the money, with certain well-known people being prepared to take up minor shareholdings and thus constitute a registered company.

The citizens of the area appear to have been taken somewhat by surprise at first, their first public intimation of what was going on being a curt paragraph in the local paper to the effect that: 'The [Hythe] Corporation has received a letter from Mr W Greenly [sic] enquiring whether a scheme for a light railway between Hythe and New Romney would have the support of the Hythe Town Council. The Town Clerk, however, has been instructed to write for further details of the proposals.'

Reading between the lines of early correspondence, it seems that the promoters were rather casual and light hearted in their initial approaches—they even received a sharp prod from the County Surveyor who wrote with some irony that he would be 'Very pleased to have any particulars that you are disposed to give me as I am somewhat interested in the matter.' Once this was realised, however, Henry Greenly in person took time off from his designing to write

*See appendix three for details.

articles and address meetings showing what was intended. On 19 September 1925, the *Folkestone Herald* was able 'through the courtesy of the Engineer and Manager' to give interesting particulars; these are quoted here since they show how the scheme developed as it went along. At this time it was intended to lay a single line only between New Romney and Hythe with two stations at Dymchurch and a halt at Jesson Camp, near Littlestone, together with sidings for ballast traffic (the Kent County Council, with extensive ballast pits at West Hythe, were interested in using the railway). Goods and parcels were to be carried and provision was to be made for doubling the line 'if required'. So eager was the paper that a week later it gaily announced the passing of a light railway order that had not then even been formally applied for! That, however, was some time off, the formal application not being made until 28 November by which time a lot of hard spade-work had been done. The preliminaries of any such legal proceedings are rather boring but it may be worth giving some idea of what had to be done to avoid substantial objections which might have caused the scheme to founder. The War Office's concern over possible incursions on their land, both at Hythe and an airstrip near Jesson, had to be soothed; a clause for the protection of the Southern Railway incorporated; and the worries of various district councils about road crossings and sewers set at rest.

THE SCHEME DEVELOPS

Meanwhile 'the scheme' had been expanding. On 23 November, Henry Greenly disclosed to a public meeting at Hythe that the line would now be double from New Romney to Dymchurch, that private sidings 'for food stuffs' would be laid at Jesson Holiday Camp, that traffic was expected to be largely passengers and some ballast. The meeting, with only one dissenter, promised its support to the proposed light railway, a procedure later repeated at various public and council meetings further down the coast. Only at Dymchurch was there some dissension. There a hastily formed Owners and Tenants Association, mainly composed of landowners affected by the proposed route, claimed to speak for the village and suggested that one of their members should represent Dymchurch at any public inquiry. A spirited meeting was held by them early in December—the main points of interest emerging from it being that a double line was now proposed, and that for the first time the question was raised of a branch to Sandling Junction. Mr Greenly did not consider it would be practicable! In any case the parish held an open meeting only a few days later and decided by a large majority to support the railway.

By the end of 1925, therefore, matters were progressing satisfactorily, with only the occasional minor setback caused by incautiousness and inexperience on the part of the promoters. It had been decided by now that an original proposal to run a 15in gauge branch across the road at New Romney to reach the Southern station (Railway No 2) would be replaced by a standard gauge connection (Railway No 3) with interchange sidings on RH & D property. This occasioned one of Henry Greenly's few gaffes when he tried to assuage the local council's opposition to the goods level crossing proposed. There would, he assured them, not need to be more than 'about four trains a day' across the road, and the council took him at his word. They demanded inclusion in the light railway order of a clause permitting 'not more than four times (two each way) daily' and nothing would shift them from that position. A clause was duly written into the LRO but since the expected interchange traffic never materialised the railway was not, in the event, embarrassed.

PUBLIC INQUIRY

The next two important events took place early in 1926. The first was the inevitable public inquiry into the application for a light railway order, which took place at Hythe early in January. The main reasons for this were that, as was usual, the promoters had not been able to satisfy all objections to their scheme, while it was the Board of Trade's duty to ensure that all safety requirements (eg at road crossings) would be met. The main objectors were the East Kent Road-Car Co, which operated bus services in the area, and various landowners along the route, notably at Dymchurch. The bus company was at the time an implacable opponent and had, indeed, declared in a letter to Greenly that it would oppose the scheme on all possible grounds. It was, very naturally, worried about the effect the railway would have on its Folkestone–Dymchurch–New Romney route. The matter was particularly important to it since the route depended for profitability on summer visitors who would certainly be attracted by the trains. Unfortunately the bus company rather spoiled its own case by suddenly reducing the rather high fares then in force, a measure it had stubbornly resisted taking for some years past; its representative did not improve matters by admitting that the railway would not affect the Folkestone–Lydd route which was 'really the paying traffic'. The New Romney service was, in any case, not popular, even the local newspaper producing a crisp editorial on how difficult it had been to get to New Romney to attend inquiry proceedings there! Evidence was also brought that the average passenger load of buses in winter on the route was only 1·7 per trip (survey during first week of January).

If the bus company had a sense of grievance, however, the landowners were more vociferous still. Semi-derelict plots throughout Dymchurch, it appeared, had great potential building value which would be seriously reduced by the smuts and noise of the railway's presence; excellent agricultural land would be ruthlessly cut in half and its usefulness thereby much dimished. All Mr Greenly's provisions for multitudinous cattle creeps and no less than thirty gated accommodation crossings would hardly, it was suggested, alleviate this disaster. No doubt most of these horror stories were produced with a very reasonable eye to obtaining maximum compensation; this was, after all, the period of the first big holiday camps and developments— Jesson and Maddieson's camps and a rash of shanty bungalows behind the sea wall. The owners slightly marred their environmental case by suggesting that if a railway was to come they wanted 'a full-size one', which presumably would have been both smuttier and noisier. Yet they did also bring some sense into the promoters' rather grandiose ideas of a second 'Sand Hutton' railway for the local farming community. Both Howey and Greenly were having visions of farm sidings sprouting at intervals, patronised by grateful farmers who would load their crops and sheep galore to save themselves trouble. The Sand Hutton was even quoted extensively as a model and Henry Greenly, on his own statement, designed the big bogie wagons (see page 142) with high slatted sides to take ten sheep apiece; the smaller wagons, he casually added, could easily be adapted to take six animals. These ideas were quite firmly disposed of by the objectors who pointed out quite gently that (i) they sold most of their goods through Hythe not Romney and Hastings, so that there would be no interchange traffic with the Southern and (ii) that, since the railway run to Hythe averaged less than four miles and they had to trans-ship twice it really would not be economic to use the railway. The ministry inspector then retired to consider his verdict, having made sure that the promoters and local councils had agreed on the thorny problem of road-crossings. In practice these were important only at two points, on the potentially busy road at West Hythe and where the railway crossed the main Hythe–New Romney road near Warren House. In both cases the railway agreed to provide tunnels under the road; the remaining crossings were over lanes only, 'Mr Greenly averring that he had planned the route with just this in mind'.

BUILDING THE LINE

'Mr Greenly' was meanwhile very involved with the first stages in actually building the railway, work having started at New Romney end well before the decision of the public inquiry was even announced. It appears that the South Eastern Railway, a predecessor of the Southern, had actually purchased land in the New Romney area about 1900 when it obtained powers for a branch extension towards Hythe. This was made available to Captain Howey by the good offices of the Southern Railway and he was thus able to buy the site of his New Romney terminus without waiting for the results of any litigation. It was at this point that the second important event took place.

Again reading between the lines, Captain Howey wanted a railway on which to drive and did not really want to be concerned with the background organisation that made such a thing possible—the minutiae of maintenance, day-to-day running etc. Henry Greenly, on the other hand, was an engineer and he was very much concerned with efficient organisation. He had an interest in a light engineering company, Jackson, Rigby Ltd, that specialised in miniature railway material and was at the time operating at Shalford in Surrey. To save the railway company having to set up its own technical organisation, it was therefore agreed that Jackson, Rigby Ltd should move its business to New Romney station, taking over certain railway buildings, bring its own skilled personnel and run the technical side under contract. This involved production and repair of equipment, provision of all the signalling apparatus, etc, the company simultaneously carrying on its normal engineering business. Indeed at the time of moving it was engaged on a contract to provide two Greenly-designed 12in gauge American-type Pacifics and rolling stock for an exhibition line in Philadephia and these were duly

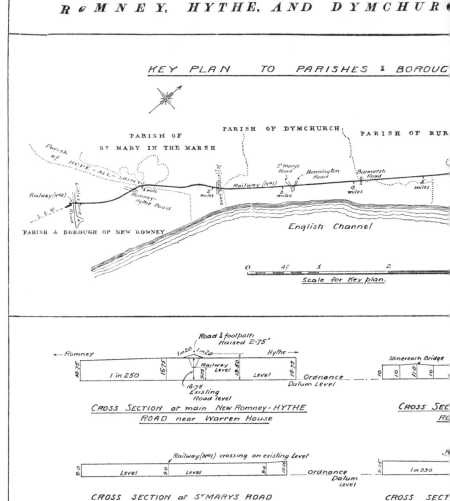

KEY PLAN TO PARISHES & BOROUC

PARISH OF DYMCHURCH

PARISH OF BUR

PARISH OF
St MARY IN THE MARSH

Parish
of HOPE ALL SAINTS

St Marys
Road
Bonnington
Road
Burmarsh
Road

Railway (Nº1)

1 mile
2 miles
3 miles
4 miles
5 miles

Railway (Nº2)

Romney-
Hythe Road

1 Milestone
S. E. Rª

PARISH & BOROUGH OF NEW ROMNEY

English Channel

0   4f   1   2

Scale for Key plan.

Road & footpath
Raised 2·75'

←Romney   1 in 20   1 in 20   Hythe→

Railway
Level

1 in 250   Level

16·75
Existing
Road level

Ordnance
Datum Level

Stonereach Bridge

CROSS SECTION at main New Romney-HYTHE
ROAD near Warren House

CROSS SEC
RO

Railway(Nº1) crossing on existing Level

Level   Level   Ordnance
Datum
Level

1 in 330

CROSS SECTION at St MARYS ROAD
DYMCHURCH

CROSS SECT
L

0   5chns   1 furlong   2 furlongs

Horizontal Scale for Sections

10 5 0 10

Vertical Scale

Overall plan for RH & DR

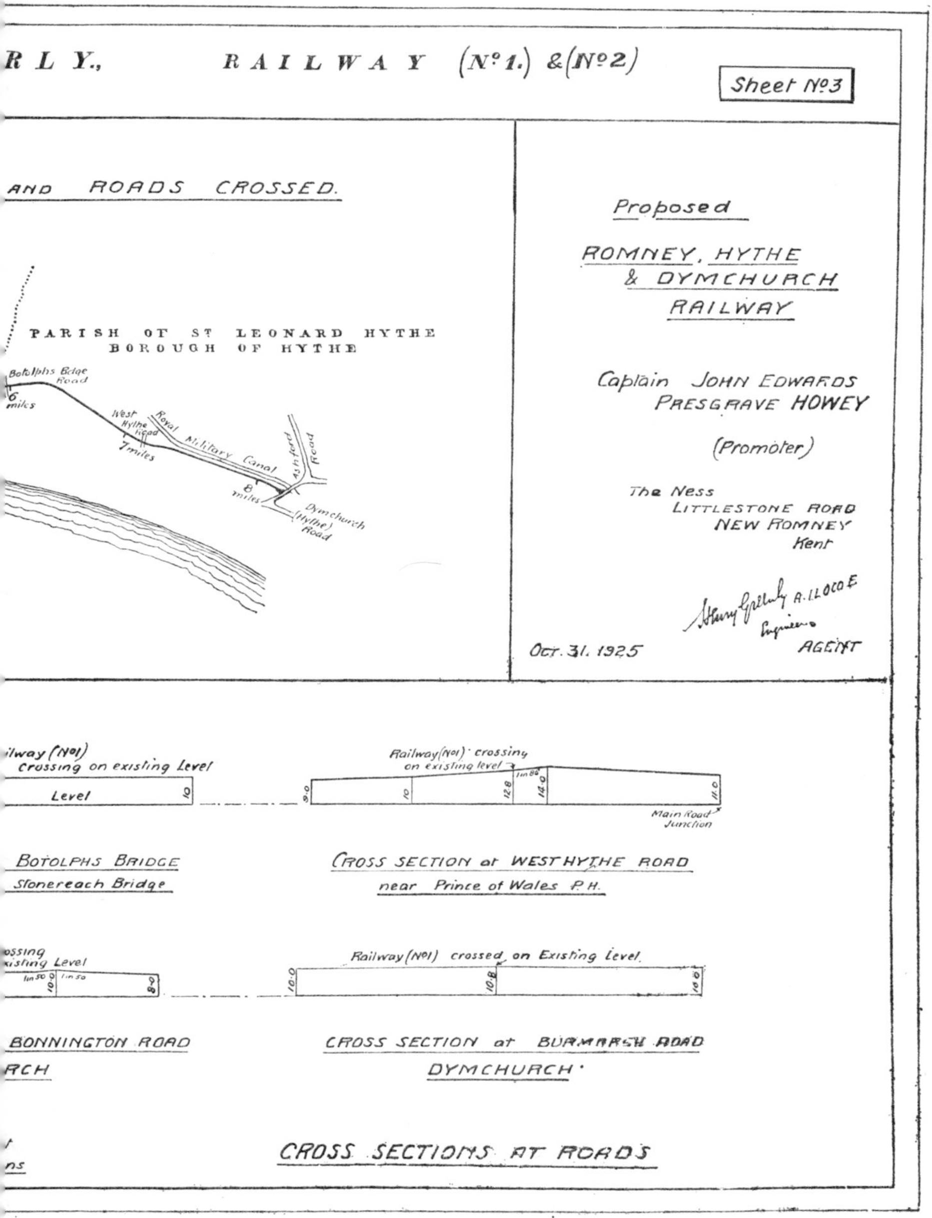

R L Y.,
RAILWAY (No 1.) & (No 2)
Sheet No 3
AND ROADS CROSSED.
PARISH OF ST LEONARD HYTHE
BOROUGH OF HYTHE
Botolphs Bdge Road
6 miles
West Hythe Road
7 miles
Royal Military Canal
Ashford Road
8 miles
Dymchurch (Hythe) Road
Proposed
ROMNEY, HYTHE & DYMCHURCH RAILWAY
Captain JOHN EDWARDS PRESGRAVE HOWEY
(Promoter)
The Ness
LITTLESTONE ROAD
NEW ROMNEY
Kent
A.I.LOCO.E
Engineer
AGENT
Oct. 31. 1925
ilway (No1) crossing on existing Level
Level
Railway (No1) crossing on existing level
Main Road Junction
BOTOLPHS BRIDGE
Stonereach Bridge
CROSS SECTION at WEST HYTHE ROAD
near Prince of Wales P.H.
ossing
xisting Level
Railway (No1) crossed on Existing Level.
BONNINGTON ROAD
RCH
CROSS SECTION at BURMARSH ROAD
DYMCHURCH
CROSS SECTIONS AT ROADS

tted to ministry for the LRO

completed and delivered. The arrangement was a most unusual one and, as will be seen, led to considerable complications after only a short period. At the time, however, it proved extremely convenient since Greenly was able to exercise direct control over the production of equipment to his designs and could modify or alter them at short notice. Construction of the necessary machine shops was pushed forward and, as soon as they were completed the 'JR Co' moved in, in stages during the autumn of 1926. Meanwhile, the legal preliminaries ground on. The result of the public inquiry, published in February, was favourable and a revised light railway order was approved in May, the Romney, Hythe & Dymchurch Light Railway Company, becoming thereby incorporated. The company was authorised to build and work its railways, Nos 1 and 3, using steam or 'such other motive power as may be authorised' but specifically not by electricity. No definite speed limit was laid down in the order but a definite schedule was attached specifying minimum weights of rail (20lb/yd for the 15in gauge) and defining the methods of securing the rails to the sleepers. The company was absolved from the need to provide turntables, and need not provide shelters and lavatories at its stations; unusually for a light railway, however, it had to provide home and distant signals and they had to be interlocked. Capital was increased from the original £25,000 to £33,000, presumably by using previously obtained borrowing powers of £8,000; this had been one of the major queries of objectors at the public inquiry, and Greenly had made much play with figures showing a probable surplus of capital over expenditure of some £55! This increase allowed, no doubt, for a considerable expansion of locomotive power and rolling stock that was envisaged; the original three locomotives—a third having been ordered early in 1926—were to be supplemented by four more, and the carriage stock was to be doubled. In addition the railway company was to acquire a small shunting locomotive ordered by Jackson, Rigby.

Initial directors of the Company were to be: Captain J. E. P. Howey, Mrs Howey, Major W. B. Bell, Henry Greenly and Captain J. A. Holder, these to continue in office until the first general meeting of the company; in practice this board was soon varied to provide a public 'face'. General Sir Ivor Maxse KCB CVO DSO became chairman and one of Howey's motor racing friends K. Lee Guinness joined the board, while Henry Greenly retired to become simply 'Engineer and Manager'. Captain Howey, though owning

99·1 per cent of the shares, contented himself with the deputy chairmanship.

With the acquisition of the light railway order, which allowed compulsory purchase of disputed lands, work was pushed forward vigorously. The two existing Pacifics were put into use hauling construction trains, New Romney station grew rapidly and rail-head was pushed out across the marsh towards Dymchurch. It may be worthwhile at this point to take a look at the company and its ideals, so that future events can be clearly seen in the light of their context.

The railway, as finally approved, was to be a double line of 8¼ miles in length, starting from a site just across the road from the Southern Railways' New Romney branch terminus. This site was actually between the twin towns of Littlestone on Sea and New Romney but a little nearer the latter. Here, comprehensive exchange facilities with the SR were planned via 'Railway No 3' with provision for trans-shipment of heavy goods, and the route then struck out across the marsh via a halt at 'Holiday Camp' for Jesson's Camp to the major intermediate station of Dymchurch (Marshlands) immediately behind Dymchurch village. Thence it served the north-east end of Dymchurch (Burmarsh Road) and turned away from the sea once more to cross the marsh and enter Hythe alongside the Royal Military Canal. The Hythe terminus was at Gallows Corner, conveniently placed for connecting bus services but some way from the centre of the town and well below and short of the SR station. The whole layout of the line shows Captain Howey's determination to run a 'real main line' railway on the 15in gauge. Not only was the track double, with quite complicated trackwork in places, but the line was to be fully signalled with starter and shunting signals as well as those stipulated by the ministry. Turntables were to be provided at New Romney, Hythe and Dymchurch, the latter place being envisaged as a genuine intermediate terminus for short work-ings and equipped with a bay platform complete with run-round loop. The plans illustrate what was to become a major misjudgement on the part of the promoters for it was obviously envisaged that the traffic centre would be New Romney. All the locomotive facilities were concentrated there, elaborate goods exchange facilities were envisaged and a four-platform station was provided to cope with the expected traffic. At Dymchurch, the terminal roads were laid out to be convenient for short workings to and from New Romney, an arrangement which proved highly inconvenient when the focus of passenger traffic turned out to be Hythe. That the carriage of goods and ballast obviously loomed large in the promoters' minds is shown by the number of wagons provided—more than *30* four-wheeled and two bogie vehicles. Greenly had, from the inception of the scheme, consistently stated that goods locomotives would be provided and it was almost certainly for this expected traffic that two 4–8–2 locomotives were ordered from Davey Paxman Ltd, (RH & D Nos 5 and 6). Once more a Romney legend—that they were ordered for the 'projected Sandling branch'—appears to have little basis in fact. Although a preliminary survey of such a line was undertaken, it seems to have been done mainly to confirm the impracticability of such a scheme. No capital was ever raised, no references made in the light railway order proceedings. All Greenly's public announcements about it throw cold water on the idea and in practice the company lost no time in arranging a bus connection which did all that was needed. The 'siding' that projected past No 1 platform at Hythe during the early years was avowedly put in to assist in the unloading of fish traffic after the railway was extended to Dungeness. In practice that traffic never materialised.

THE DUKE OF YORK'S VISIT

In mid-1926, however, Hythe was still a considerable distance away. Indeed at the beginning of August there was a slight panic to get the line built as far as 'Holiday Camp' since the Duke of York was visiting the children's camp there which he sponsored; he had expressed a desire to travel on the new railway and the management was only too ready to oblige. The major engineering work of the line was a 56ft span 'N' girder bridge near the camp and this was completed just in time for the duke's visit. The six four-wheeled coaches that had been completed were coupled to several wagons to provide a train and on 5 August *Northern Chief* propelled them up from New Romney and onto the bridge where one track had been laid. The duke mounted the footplate accompanied by Captain Howey with Mr (later Sir) Nigel Gresley, whose GN Pacifics had been the inspiration for Greenly's design, riding on the rear of the tender and the train, laden with distinguished guests, steamed triumphantly to the New Romney terminus. After suitable jollifications it then returned to the camp to deposit its exalted passengers. Following this excitement, work continued in building the line towards Hythe. Dymchurch was reached early in the autumn and it was confidently predicted that Christmas would see rails laid into Hythe station.

There was obviously more delay than expected since it was not until the beginning of February 1927 that the railway company formally applied to Hythe corporation for permission to build its tunnel under the road at West Hythe; to be more precise it built a bridge over the railway, half the road width at a time; meanwhile guaranteeing the town council against any accidents that might occur. Two more locomotives were delivered in the spring being No 3, a Pacific similar to the original, and No 5, a 4–8–2 which was effectively a small-wheeled elongation of the *original* design; as the *Railway Magazine* put it in Irish fashion, it was 'very similar except for essential differences'. Both these engines were delivered unnamed although photographs taken at Davey Paxman's works show No 3 as *Southern Chief*. In practice they were soon named *Southern Maid* and *Hercules* respectively, although the names were not affixed until late 1927, but meanwhile they were followed by another 4–8–2 No 6 *Sampson* and two further Pacifics Nos 7 *Typhoon* and 8 *Hurricane*. These latter were three-cylinder machines with a Greenly designed valve gear to the inside cylinder and were undoubtedly the Captain's pride and joy. For them to pull, a total of sixty four-wheeled semi-open coaches was provided in a handsome dark green and white livery, together with a fair selection of goods vehicles. All locomotives were fitted with vacuum brakes and the passenger stock was either piped or braked.

COMPLETION

By July the railway was complete and had been formally inspected and approved by the Ministry of Transport. Unusually for a 'light railway' the inspector was *very* favourably impressed, declaring that the company had provided a 'main-line' installation and therefore had his blessing to operate it as such. In practice this meant that no undue speed restrictions were imposed except at the ungated level crossings. The railway was now ready for its formal opening, which took place on 16 July, but it may be worth mentioning that this was not the first revenue earning trip. Since the beginning of the 1927

holiday season 'Saturday specials' had been run between New
Romney and the Duke of York's camp at Jesson to carry the children
holidaying there. Since no turn-round facilities existed at Jesson,
the trains ran on light to Dymchurch and there were turned and
serviced before their return.

CHAPTER 3

The Early Years

OPENING

As befitted a company with such an impressive-sounding board of directors, the Romney Hythe and Dymchurch Railway was opened with considerable pomp on Saturday 16 July 1927. No less a person than the Lord Warden of the Cinque Ports, Earl Beauchamp KG, came down in full regalia to flatter the company's promoter and declare 'this unique railway' open. There were the usual speeches during which the local people were urged to support the line by using it both as passengers and for goods. Earl Beauchamp said it showed the Cinque Ports flair for combining old and new. Sir Ivor Maxse introduced it as 'the most sporting railway in the whole world . . . chiefly because it has been built by sportsmen', and said nice things about its promoters—though Captain Howey may have been a little startled at being described as 'a fairy with a golden wand'! No doubt, however, he was relieved to hear Earl Beauchamp say that 'I am glad I have not been asked to drive the first train as it would have resulted in the first accident'. Having thus relieved the feelings of those present, the Earl then 'declared the line open to the public by pressing an electric button which dropped the signals to the "All clear" position'. Since Greenly's signalling was strictly mechanical and interlocked, what he presumably did was to ring a bell in the signal box whereupon someone pulled the appropriate signal off!

The official party then took their seats in the special train of 20 four-wheeled coaches, drawn by 4–8–2 No 5. 'The powerful little engine in the front gave a shrill whistle, got rid of some surplus steam and then quickly got going. We were off' as the much impressed reporter wrote. The newspaper account of the opening is too long to quote in full, although worth reading for connoisseurs of such articles if only for the way that a crisp account of the timetable blends straight into some inconsequent notes on the best way of using the pedals on a pianoforte; editors had to be versatile in those days and use up every inch of space! Of interest is the fact that no less than six intermediate stations or halts were in use from the opening, additional ones being provided by Prince of Wales Bridge, Botolph's Bridge crossing and the Warren Bridge. A bus service was provided between Hythe (Light Railway Station) and Sandling Junction.

There were some revenue earning trains on the opening Saturday but regular services commenced the following day. For such a small railway the timetable was extremely good, the first trains of the day leaving New Romney at 6.30am and Hythe at 7.15am, while the last train left Hythe as late as 9.30 in the evening. Users were promised that when ministry lighting regulations had been met trains would run as late as 11.00pm. This was on the authority of one G. D. Bellamy who was named as the general manager. As Henry Greenly was still 'Manager and Engineer', Bellamy presumably saw to the day-to-day running of the line; he was assisted in this as traffic manager by a colourful character called Robert Hardie, who had been enticed away from the Eskdale line where he held a similar post. Hardie had long been associated with Greenly through Bassett-Lowke and Proctor Mitchell, who were among the pioneers of 15in gauge scale railways. His own main claim to fame was as a champion barber —he was reputed to have won an international shaving competition in Chicago some years before—but he was on the Eskdale line described as 'a good working foreman' and he appears to have been such at New Romney. Certainly he soon got elected to Hythe council and settled down with the railway.

EARLY CHANGES AND PROBLEMS

Indeed any other railway would also have settled down for a bit after the confusion of its construction but not the 'Romney'. The following two years were perhaps the most eventful in its life, both as regards changes in the line itself and in the personalities controlling it.

Both Howey and Greenly were clearly not content with what they had done so far. As early as 20 August, only a month after the opening, Henry Greenly gave a talk to the local Rotary Club in which he raised the idea of a proposed extension to Dungeness. In the course

Page 35 (above) *New Romney in 1926, on the day of the Duke of York's visit. Red Tiles can be seen rising in the right background while the locomotive depot is under construction behind the signal box; (below) New Romney locomotive depot as built. To the left is 'Don's Hut', in the centre the locomotive shed and to the right the machine shops*

Page 36 *New Romney. The only good view of the trans-shipment yard, in 1928–9.*
The high level loading bank can be clearly seen

of the talk he also let fall scraps of useful information such as that the Sandling extension was not seriously being considered and that goods traffic had not come up to expectations; the only real traffic was between New Romney and Dymchurch and this was mainly in coal for local use. It is an interesting sidelight on Greenly's original concept of the railway that he boasted of the terminal stations as being 'miniature Waterloos'—presumably on the basis of their separate arrival and departure platforms, scissors crossovers and impressive signal gantries. The vision of both Howey and Greenly was obviously one of a busy main line railway throughout, with plenty of trains and a general air of bustle.

Unfortunately, it very soon became clear that, to some extent, this very ambitious and delightful scheme in itself introduced defects into the design of the railway. To pack the requisite trackage into the space available, Greenly had designed point work of down to 125ft radius and had incorporated scissors crossovers of this radius at both Hythe and New Romney, together with a number of vital turnouts. In practice even the Pacifics found these difficult to negotiate while the 4-8-2s, with their longer wheelbase, became a positive embarrassment. Both scissors crossovers were consequently lifted within a year and replaced by pairs of larger radius crossovers but many siding points had to remain. In consequence, as will be described later, the two 4-8-2s were very little used during the 1920s and 1930s and, indeed, became semi-derelict; presumably the other misjudgement regarding goods traffic rendered them largely unnecessary.

Other defects arose mainly from the 'state of the art' at the time. Henry Greenly was undoubtedly one of the foremost model engineers of his time but his origins were in miniature railways of the Bassett-Lowke garden variety. Hence the original summer coaches designed for the railway were semi-open four-wheelers which proved not entirely suitable for the long runs, and exposed country. In spite of a low centre of gravity and long wheelbase they had a tendency to 'hunt' at speed, the sides open above the waist gave little protection from the wind and rain, and the need for luggage and guard space was surprisingly almost entirely overlooked. Several van bodies had to be constructed somewhat hurriedly at New Romney during the summer of 1927 to remedy this deficiency! Perhaps it is not entirely fair to criticise with hindsight but Sir Arthur Heywood had, many years previously, established the desirability of bogie coaches and since only half the four-wheelers had vacuum brakes although all had

C

through pipes, they had to be close coupled in pairs to provide adequate braking power. Additionally, Henry Greenly himself had already realised the need for closed vehicles suitable for winter use and had talked of Heywood-type vehicles. He now (summer 1927) resurrected his plans for a set of handsome 12-seater compartment bogie coaches equipped with steam heating and electric light and with luggage compartments over the bogies. Eight were built by the Clayton Carriage & Wagon Company during the winter of 1927–8 and set a new standard of comfort for the 15in gauge. They also set a new fashion in livery, being turned out in a new livery of chocolate and cream with gold lettering shaded blue. For some reason this was officially considered 'more dignified' than the original green and the four-wheelers were progressively repainted as they came in for modification.

The modifications, which took place during the 1928–9 seasons, consisted of partially enclosing the vehicles above the waist with side windows and of fitting detachable, celluloid upper panels to the door openings.

THE DUNGENESS EXTENSION

If the company had to a limited extent 'jumped the gun' when building its original line, it did not even wait for starter's orders when once decided on an extension to Dungeness. It must be appreciated that Dungeness in those days was not the seaside development it is now. Beyond 'The Pilot' public house there was no made up road, and no development; the local fishermen transacted their business on plank 'shingle shoes' known as back-stays and used rough tramways to trolley their catches to a point whence they could be collected by lorry. The lighthouse keepers and coast-guards received their supplies from the Southern Railway's branch of a branch that left the New Romney line near Lydd and ended in the shadow of Dungeness lighthouse. From its terminus a long siding trailed down to the fishing beach and a primitive weigh-house; it was used mainly for obtaining shingle ballast. Hence there were not likely to be many objections and most of the land required—then virtually worthless—was obtained by private negotiation. By the end of January 1928, half the six miles odd had been laid, three stations were being built and a tunnel was being constructed under the road at New Romney, presumably with the full agreement of the local council. The stations were named as being at Great Stones Dunes

[sic], then the subject of a new holiday development, The Pilot, and Dungeness itself . . . It was not until February that formal application for the necessary light railway order was made and work went busily on during the eight weeks in which the LRO announcement had by law to be continued. Powers were specifically sought, among other things, for using i/c engined locomotives, an indication that winter traffic was not proving very fruitful.

The public inquiry into the new application for a light railway order was held on 18 March 1928 at New Romney town hall. Unlike the previous one it was all very amicable and it is clear that it was no more than a formality. There were only three objectors and their complaints had been met by the time the inquiry opened; Trinity House was worried about buildings obstructing the light, a matter which was easily settled. The Southern intended to modify the course of its New Romney branch to serve Greatstone and feared the RH & D might block its access; Howey promptly re-routed his line further towards the coast; Mr Fork of 'The Old Battery' asked for and obtained compensation for use of his land. Otherwise everyone was in favour; the line, after all, would help the fishermen considerably and would, it was said, provide rapid transport for coastguard apparatus in times of emergency. The Board of Trade even sent a representative down to support the application on these grounds. The Inspector duly retired to complete his report but the result was such a foregone conclusion that the local paper did not even bother to report it. The extension had reached 'The Pilot' by the middle of May and was opened as far as that point on 24 May. One delay in reaching Dungeness lighthouse was apparently due to a difficulty in finding a sufficiently firm route on which to lay the track among shifting shingle. Greenly was forced to deviate from his original route, this requiring negotiation with the Dungeness Estate from whom the land for this final portion was leased.

Meanwhile all trains terminated at—or rather just before—'The Pilot' for part of the 1928 summer season. Since this was only a temporary terminus it was not thought worthwhile providing a turntable, a construction rendered difficult in any case by the shingly nature of the area. A large turning wye was therefore laid out about 300yd short of 'The Pilot' public house, extending inland from the double-track main line (see plan in appendix five) and thus enabling locomotives to be turned. The procedure was to leave the train on the 'down-line' while the locomotive ran round the wye and then

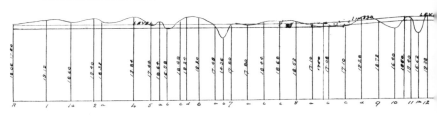

LEVELS AROUND LOOP.

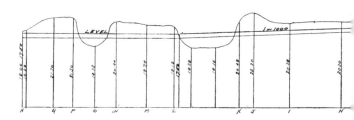

LEVELS FROM No. 1 BATTERY TO COMMENCEMENT OF LOOP.

R. H. & D. Rly.
DUNGENESS EXTENSION.

Gradient profile of levels ro

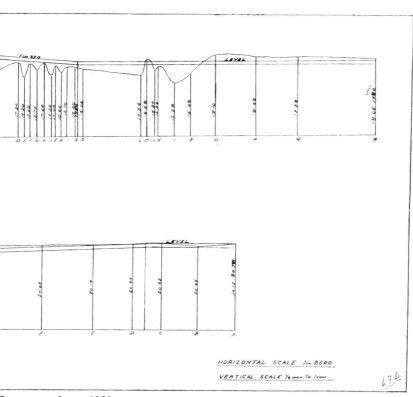

HORIZONTAL SCALE 1 in 2500

VERTICAL SCALE ⅛ inch to 1 foot

Dungeness loop, 1929

back down over a trailing crossover; meanwhile the passengers amused themselves, or bought tickets from a temporary wooden booking office hut.

The exact date of opening through to Dungeness has long been disputed, mainly because the printed timetables did not show trains throughout until September 1928 while various articles referred to trains running through at least during the 1928/9 winter service. It has now been established that through trains started running at August bank holiday weekend without any ceremony and that the wye was very soon lifted.

From The Pilot onwards, the line ran—and still runs—on land which belongs to the Dungeness Estate but over which the railway has the right in perpetuity to run its trains; a rather unusual arrangement. To avoid unnecessary shunting, the end of the line was made in the form of a huge balloon loop, Dungeness station standing on the southernmost curve; the station buildings had been completed some time before the line reached them and their layout, with the shelter and signalbox lying at a slightly diverging angle from the track, rather indicate that a simple dead-end terminus was originally contemplated.

All trains ran round this loop clockwise, automatically passing from down to up track without any pointwork. A short stock siding was provided very soon after opening and a profuse array of signals although the latter were hardly necessary, did not weather well and were soon removed. The whole extension was double-tracked throughout, except for the loop, and initially was fully signalled.

FURTHER ALTERATIONS

Concurrently with the building of the Dungeness extension—and in some cases influenced by it—a number of changes took place on the existing parts of the railway. Some were logical developments. In the spring of 1928 an asphalted car park was laid in at Hythe station since 'up to 50 cars a day' were wishing to park there, and No 1 road was extended into the forecourt towards Scanlons Bridge (see sketches in appendix five) to ease trans-shipment for the expected fish traffic; it will be seen that no real provision for goods traffic had been made at Hythe.

Working along the line from Hythe towards New Romney, there were several ephemeral features. Just by the road bridge at West

Hythe a shelterless halt, Prince of Wales Halt, was provided soon after the opening but was little used and was closed in 1928. (The bridge and halt, it must be said, were not named after the Prince of Wales, to 'balance' the Duke of York's Bridge, so to speak, but were so called after a nearby public house!) About a mile further on a long temporary siding, facing to New Romney was installed on the seaward side early in 1927 to allow shingle ballast to be taken from an existing bank. It was not used after the opening so far as is known but the disconnected rails survived until about 1937. At Botolph's Bridge a shelter and cinder platform were provided, though of little apparent use since the area was devoid of housing, while Burmarsh Road, at the north end of Dymchurch, was early provided with substantial buildings and signals.

The major modifications to track and fittings, however, took place at New Romney, which had to be tranformed, within six months of its opening, from a terminus to a through station. Here, to the frustrated historian, buildings and tracks seem to have been moved frequently and often apparently overnight (since no detailed plans appear to have existed it has been extremely difficult to delineate the original layout).

This appears to have been that shown in appendix five. The station was intended to be the focal point for traffic so had both arrival and departure platforms for passenger trains. It also contained the loco-motive and carriage sheds together with machine shops for Jackson, Rigby Ltd and what was intended to be a fairly elaborate goods trans-shipment layout with loading bank and goods shed. There is no evidence that the latter was ever completely brought into use but merchandise was being carried in 1928 (314 tons for the year) and the facilities could not therefore be destroyed when the Dungeness extension was being considered. A rather unsatisfactory layout had, therefore, to be adopted in which the main line, curving in past the carriage and wagon shops, negotiated an S bend to run down into a new low level station. By propping up the interchange facilities with a vertical retaining wall, and by removing one track of the old terminal portion, there was just room for the double track main line and a single long narrow platform on the down (Dungeness) side. The up platform, complete with buildings, had perforce to be constructed on the far side of Littlestone Road, squeezed between the rails and the boundary of the SR station; a footbridge was provided to give access both to the SR station and to a dirt track giving onto Littlestone

ROMNEY HYTHE & DYMCHURCH L
RAILWAY N°4 EXTENSION: NEW RO
SITUATED IN THE PARISHES & BOROUGHS OF

SHEET

DENGE BEACH

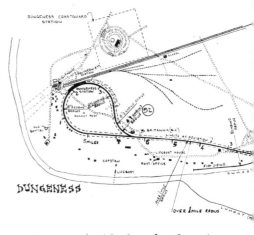

DUNGENESS COASTGUARD
STATION

DUNGENESS
STATION

DUNGENESS

STRAIT

10 CHAINS 0   10   20   30   40   50

HORIZONTAL SCALE FOR PLANS AND SECTIONS: SCALE SIX INCHES

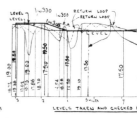

ALL LEVELS IN FEET ABOVE ORDNANCE DATUM   LEVELS TAKEN AND CHECKED F

COMPLETED PLAN
ROMNEY HYTHE & DYMCHURCH LIGHT RAILWAY

The final form of the Dungeness loop
simply show

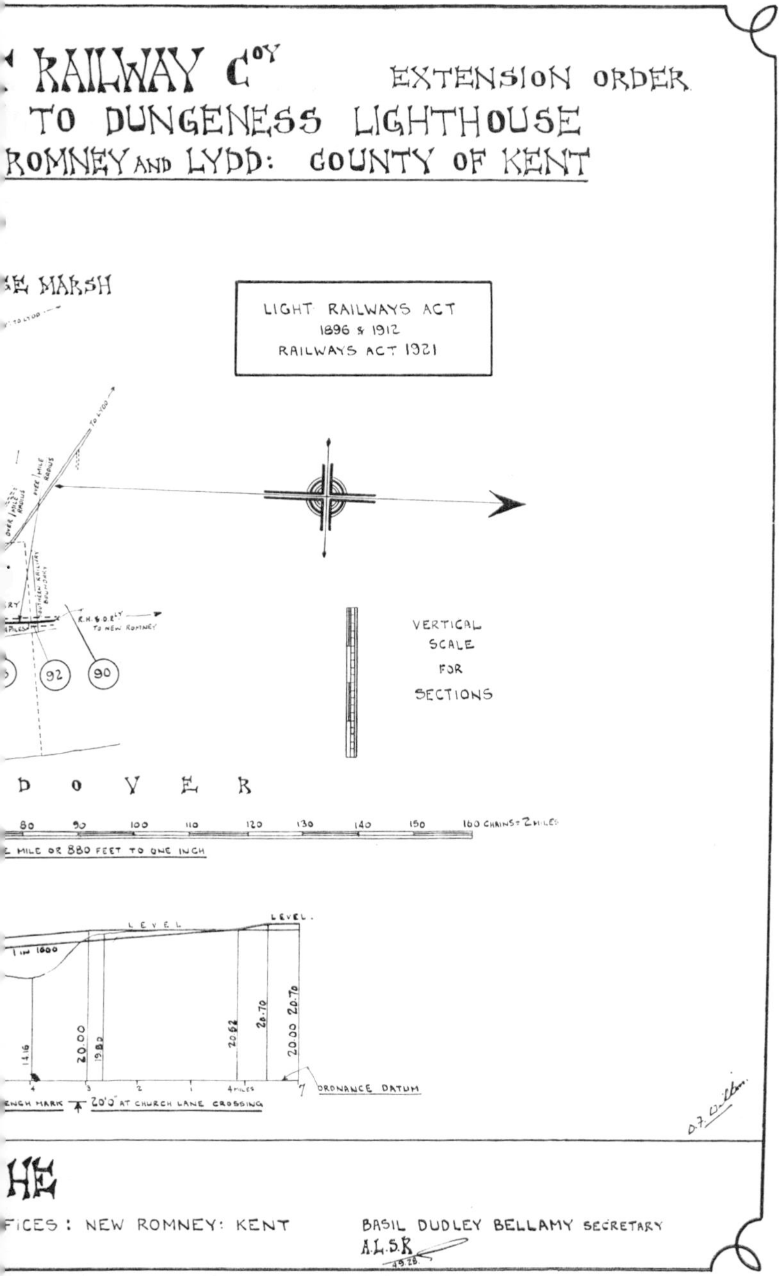

RAILWAY C^OY
EXTENSION ORDER
TO DUNGENESS LIGHTHOUSE
ROMNEY AND LYDD: COUNTY OF KENT
E MARSH
LIGHT RAILWAYS ACT
1896 & 1912
RAILWAYS ACT 1921
TO LYDD
R.H. & D.R^LY TO NEW ROMNEY
92
90
VERTICAL SCALE FOR SECTIONS
D O V E R
80 90 100 110 120 130 140 150 160 CHAINS = 2 MILES
E MILE OR 880 FEET TO ONE INCH
LEVEL
LEVEL.
1 in 1600
14.16
20.00
19.80
20.62
20.70
20.00 20.70
4 MILES
ORDNANCE DATUM
ENCH MARK
20'0" AT CHURCH LANE CROSSING
HE
FICES: NEW ROMNEY: KENT
BASIL DUDLEY BELLAMY SECRETARY
A.L.S.R.

g the fish siding inserted; earlier plans
n for a siding

Road and the main booking office. Although a later Romney legend claimed this layout was to give all trains a start on the down grade— the line had to dip to pass beneath Littlestone Road—it was obviously inconvenient and uneconomical in staff and the arrangement lasted only for about two years. Meanwhile the station was officially re-named Littlestone-on-Sea to fit in with the Southern Railway's desire to publicise its coastal branches by officially terminating them at resorts.

GREENLY FALLS OUT WITH HOWEY

It might be thought that the railway was now complete and could settle down to a period of consolidation but this was not so. There was increasing friction between Henry Greenly and Captain Howey over a number of factors affecting the line, culminating in what by all accounts was a blazing row. Its origin lay almost certainly in the characters of the two men, and, ironically, in their very devotion to the railway both had done so much to bring into being. Howey was rich, mildly eccentric in some ways, and very much accustomed to having his own way. He, quite naturally, having conceived and paid for the line, considered it as *his* railway to do what he liked with. He was very much an enthusiast for miniature railways but not, it appears, much concerned about the mundane details of construction and maintenance—that was what general managers were appointed for. Greenly, on the other hand, having, so to speak, given birth to the railway, no doubt considered it in many ways as *his*. He had after all designed almost everything from the track and fittings to the rolling stock, had undertaken all the legal work of obtaining a light railway order and negotiating the various contracts and had supervised the construction of the line. He had even persuaded his fellow directors in the Jackson, Rigby company—Howey, J. A. Holder, and G. B. Chaldecott—to move the company to New Romney so that the railway had its own supervised source of material and labour. Indeed Chaldecott became the works manager.

Perhaps in the end it was this move that brought about the break between the two men. While the very exciting work of constructing the railway was going on, they could work in harmony and the presence of the Jackson, Rigby company was a great advantage. Once the railway was complete, however, and the Captain wanted to operate it as a showpiece, Jackson, Rigby became something of an annoyance. To start with it was a model engineering business with a wide range of standard products and it wanted to continue making these. Unfortunately they were made on a production-line basis and every time an employee was taken away for railway business the firm's main work was disorganised. Thus to the firm the railway and its constant changes must have become something of an irritation even while it provided a good deal of work. To the Captain, on the other hand, the presence of a semi-autonomous company on his property was no doubt something of an irritation too. In addition, once the Dungeness extension was operating, the railway's requirements changed from production of new items to a succession of fiddly maintenance jobs. The situation was probably exacerbated by the fact that several of Greenly's ideas had not worked out quite as well as he had hoped. In particular the long-wheelbase 4–8–2s proved baulky over the rather small radius pointwork and the four-wheeled coaches, though well up to the miniature railway standards of the time, proved not entirely suitable for the fast long-distance runs to which they were subjected; their open design, too, was not right for the driving wind and rain to be found quite frequently on the marsh and within two years of the opening they had had to be modified with additional windows and door-screens. It is quite likely that Howey would express dis-satisfaction over such points, and Greenly, although by all accounts a charming man to his equals and employees, had a reputation for being very difficult with 'superiors' whose opinions he did not respect. He certainly had a habit of standing on his dignity as a consulting engineer and was absolutely adamant about retaining copyright in any of his designs, no matter for whom they had been prepared. He had previously had a furious dispute with the Ravenglass & Eskdale Railway over the use of *Colossus* drawings when they were 'designing' the Pacific *Sir Aubrey Brocklebank*, a dispute which came very near to a court action before all parties were satisfied. It appears that a similar incident may well have been the final breaking point at Romney.

In the Summer of 1928, the Captain decided to solve the problem of Jackson, Rigby Ltd by simply buying the firm out and turning its plant over to the railway's own use. There appears to have been some altercation with his fellow directors about the price but finally agreement was reached. Production of the JR standard parts was taken over by a former employee and moved to Brighton; at New Romney Captain Howey decided that the works facilities should be used to build two new locomotives, in substitution for two *Green*

Goddess-type Pacifics that were actually on order from Davey Paxman. These were to become the Canadian outline Pacifics and their genesis raises some intriguing points. For one thing with completion of the Dungeness section, Henry Greenly had almost severed his active connection with the railway and was at this time living in his bungalow nearby working on his own model business. It is uncertain, therefore, what hand he had in their design. Certainly earlier in the year he had talked of an idea for 'American-style' locomotives, citing as advantages their ease of maintenance and better cab protection. On the other hand, Howey had a great admiration for Canadian designers and may well have simply ordered the works to produce a Canadian outline machine based on the original English Pacifics. Wheel castings, cylinders and other major items were available from Paxman's—indeed they may already have been in hand for the cancelled 1928 order—and the boilers were certainly not of Greenly design. They were ordered by Captain Howey himself after two visits to Krauss of Munich and were unmistakably designed by Roland Martens of that company. They bear all the hallmarks of his design, being in effect developments of boilers produced for *his* earlier 1925–6 Pacifics.

The suggestion that the CPRs, as they were always known, just 'grew' rather than being designed from scratch is supported by the fact that no drawings were available at the start. Indeed it may be worthwhile putting to rest the long-standing legend of 'the Greenly Drawings'. From recollections of the staff at the time it appears that there came a time when various castings had been machined, the boilers had arrived from Krauss and there rose the question 'what are these things going to look like?'. Chassis design was simple; the existing Pacific could be taken as a model with the minor modifications needed to substitute a truck for radial axleboxes. The chief draughtsman, A. S. Richardson, was therefore commissioned by Captain Howey to work up a suitable general arrangement drawing. This was nearly completed when it disappeared from his drawing board one night early in 1929; its disappearance was a mystery.

Howey was in Australia at the time and the railway management called in the police. Their suspicions obviously pointed to Greenly since his house was searched on a warrant and he was arrested but released on bail almost immediately. When the case came up in the local magistrates' court, the railway company had to admit that it had no evidence and withdrew its case, Greenly being granted an absolute discharge with costs. He subsequently entered writs against both the railway, for malicious prosecution, and Jackson, Rigby Engineering Co, but they were settled out of court. Reading between the lines, there was obviously friction of some standing between Greenly and the railway's management, in particular G. D. Bellamy whom Howey had brought in as general manager. It must have been galling for Greenly, who had done most of the creative work, to have someone supersede him in control of the railway, especially a man with his own clear ideas on how the railway should be run. At the same time Bellamy was directly responsible to Howey for ensuring that the railway ran smoothly and one can understand his point of view!

Regrettably, however, the whole incident did have two sad consequences. Henry Greenly obviously felt his mere presence might cause both him and others embarrassment and so, at the end of February 1929, he left New Romney for good. Captain Howey on his return decided that the Jackson, Rigby affair had better be concluded once and for all; the finished parts of the two CPRs were packed off summarily to the Yorkshire Engine Company for completion and the New Romney works was progressively run down. No more new construction was undertaken at New Romney and, without definitive drawings, the Yorkshire Engine Company appears to have completed the two locomotives 'by eye', taking two years to do so. Certainly to this day they differ from each other in significant details.

In retrospect it seems almost inevitable that two such fairly strong personalities would clash once their common aim was achieved. Their day to day interests were so different. Greenly was an engineer, fascinated by the design and constructional problems of the 15in gauge. Howey wanted to run his railway with minimum bother of the technical side. That Greenly envisaged permanent association with the railway is clear from the way that he designed and built a bungalow for himself as well as for Captain Howey. That he eventually had to leave was certainly the railway's loss.

GREENLY'S ACHIEVEMENT

Greenly's achievement was considerable, and in the author's opinion, has never been given the credit it deserves. It has been said that Greenly left his stamp on everything about the railway and his handiwork is still visible everywhere today, in spite of all the changes. The locomotives are, of course, the most obvious thing to catch the casual visitor's eye, but even a cursory glance at track and fittings is enough to show the original unity of design. His character- istic signals have gone recently, replaced by colour lights, but it is possible immediately to recognise his neat wooden buildings with their small gable finials. Even more basic is the enduring nature of his civil engineering works. Henry Greenly was something of a pioneer in the use of reinforced concrete and his aptitude for using this material was widely acknowledged in civil engineering journals of the period. His characteristic work in its large-stoned but enduring aggregate can still be seen in every major structure. Even where shelters and other structures have long disappeared their foundations are instantly recognisable as 'Greenly's' work. Certainly the Captain lost no time in correcting some of Greenly's errors. On the other hand, he also retained the many good items and they have shown the lasting worth of many of Greenly's ideas.

CHAPTER 4

The 1930s

YET MORE CHANGES

Henry Greenly's departure from New Romney appears to have had a cathartic affect on the railway's owner. Certainly within the next two years yet further drastic changes took place, and it is difficult to avoid the implication that Captain Howey was determined to 'put right' all the things in which he and Greenly had disagreed—and in which Greenly, as the expert, usually had his way. Some action was taken almost immediately, during the winter and spring of 1929; various realignments were realised, notably near the Warren, at Duke of York's Bridge and on the approach to Hythe. Jackson, Rigby Ltd was firmly assimilated into the railway company and its staff progressively run down to three men and a boy for general fitting and shed work. A reappraisal appears to have been made of whether the elaborate signalling and other 'main line' arrangements were really justified, with the result that Greatstone station was never completed, while the installations there and at other places on the Dungeness route in particular were allowed to fall gradually into disuse over the next couple of years. Dymchurch was still recognised as a principal intermediate station but again its facilities were reduced, the branch bay being singled and the turntable removed. Henceforth all short workings, increasingly from the Hythe direction, ran tender first in one direction or ran through as empty stock to New Romney or Hythe as appropriate. Nonetheless, the changes were not all retrospective. In preparation for future alterations at New Romney, a two-road wooden shed was erected by the turntable at Hythe and for the 1929 season appears to have been leased to the War Department. The WD was at this period beginning experiments with sound-location equipment, an ancestor of radar, and was erecting large concrete reflectors at various points on the marsh, just past Maddieson's Camp where two small dish reflectors and a large oblong parabolic 'mirror' were constructed. To serve this site a long siding was put in just past Maddieson's with a trailing connection to the up main line. The WD had running powers over the railway during the night hours and in the winter and it is almost certain that the sudden—and short lived—increase in goods traffic during 1929 was in connection with this work. The total jumped from 312 tons in 1928 to 891 tons in 1929, and since it then returned to a level of 314 tons for 1931 (no 1930 returns are available), it is a reasonable guess that WD materials via New Romney accounted for much of the increase. The WD retained running powers over this line until after the war and its maintenance staff built or acquired a small petrol scooter which was housed by day in Hythe shed. It appears probable, also, that WD winter occupation of the up line was the reason for seasonal single line working over the Dungeness extension during the early 1930s, there being evidence that for several years the balloon loop was linked into the down line during each winter by a set of points kept on site.

The year 1929 also saw various other innovations, in particular the acquisition of another crude petrol tractor for use on light passenger workings and winter trains, and various continuing modifications to stock. It is not proposed here to detail all the minor alterations which are described in chapters eight, nine and ten, but there was one further upheaval at New Romney which cannot be ignored. The botched 'rebuild' caused by the Dungeness extension was proving inconvenient in many ways and was highlighted by the rapid increase in passenger traffic. During winter 1929–30 the station area was therefore modified to ease operation. Basically, the entire up-side works was swept away, the old paint shop being cut down and re-erected as a carriage shed over the former terminal arrival platforms while carriage depot No 1 disappeared completely. The approaches from the Hythe end were realigned to remove an awkward reverse curve and to ease the down gradient into the station. A two-road erecting shop was put up at the north end almost opposite the engine shed and a resited approach to the goods yard allowed a short up platform to be squeezed in north of the up-side retaining wall. This in turn allowed abandonment of the 'new' up station sited south of Littlestone Road which had proved very inconvenient in use, and the whole ensemble was finished off by an ornamental rock garden

Page 53 (above) *A view of New Romney about 1928, looking towards Dungeness. Note the two different patterns of four-wheeler on the left, with the Social Club rising behind; (below) Hythe station, in 1928. In the train are Clayton Pullmans in their original condition; mica side-screens and the central glass partitions are visible in the four-wheelers to the left*

Page 54 (above) *Dymchurch station, August 1927. Note the temporary booking office, the 4–8–2 without nameplates, and the lack of any tea-room building;* (below) *The wooden shelter at Botolph's Bridge, seen from a down train*

complete with windmill which covered the scars of the old up-side buildings. An overall roof later covered part of the station area.

In general, the early 1930s were years of consolidation, what changes there were being mainly the result of the Greenly aftermath. The railway's discovery in 1930 of the Gibbins bogie, designed for colonial use, led first to the rebogieing of the Claytons and some tenders, Greenly's bogies having proved rather poor riding; subsequently it was decided to articulate the four-wheelers into sets of nine and five coaches using Gibbins bogies as the link and this was carried out in batches from winter 1930–31. It is not certain if all were converted. The small shunting engine, now surplus to requirements, was sold along with a few coaches and the delivery of the CPRs in 1931 allowed the two 4–8–2s to be virtually withdrawn from service. A further sharp drop in goods traffic, to 110 tons in the following year, probably sealed their fate for both were stored; *Hercules* remained largely intact but *Samson* was used as a spare parts dump and by the mid-1930s was reduced to a mere shell stored in the open by the locomotive shed.

Various other things disappeared about that time too, as the railway adjusted to its role of summer passenger carrier for tourists. This is not to say that everything went into decline; a regular winter service was provided between New Romney and Hythe right up to the war, with three trains daily on Mondays to Fridays and extra trains on Saturdays, two of these being extended to Dungeness. Captain Howey even provided a 'new' petrol locomotive for these trains in 1930, comprising the working parts of his Rolls Royce shooting brake mounted on a rail chassis. He provided new stock, too, no less than 54 very comfortable eight-seater saloons and two matching vans being delivered in 1934–5 largely to replace the unsatisfactory articulated sets. They were, for their period, superlatively equipped coaches, with fully upholstered seats, wind-down door windows and an almost excessive amount of leg-room and the railway was correspondingly proud of them. Indeed when first delivered they were specially reserved for passengers making the full round trip to Dungeness and back.

The early1930s, however, were also notable for two other features; they were the depression years which meant that even the Romney

D

had to economise in places; and they saw the rapid expansion of motor transport. It was these factors that led to the disappearance of various Romney landmarks.

First to go were probably the goods shed and trans-shipment sidings. The exact date is not known but by 1934 general goods traffic was down to 115 tons and that was the last year in which it was recorded so winter 1934–5 was the most likely time. The removal allowed the cutting through New Romney station to be opened out slightly and low-level sidings were laid on the goods yard site; most of the four-wheelers were scrapped here during the ensuing two years, robbed of their bogies for use under the new saloons.

Most of the intermediate stations also fell into disuse or decay at about this time. Burmarsh Road, Greatstone, and The Pilot gradually became unstaffed and began to look distinctly 'tatty'. There had never been any noticeable traffic at the original 'halts' and, apart form Lade, only Botolph's Bridge lingered on, finally perishing in flames by Captain Howey's own hand one night just before the war. New Romney itself, which had been 'metamorphosed' into 'Littlestone on Sea for New Romney' during the excitement over the Dungeness extension, somehow returned to its old name by the mid-1930s. There was still a down-side nameboard proclaiming it to be 'Littlestone' in 1934 and it was so described on timetables until the war but a warped 'New Romney' nameboard was in position by 1936 and the station appears locally still to have been known as New Romney except for 1928–30 or thereabouts.

There is no doubt that even the Romney had less money to throw about during the 1930s. The stations gradually got less smart, the track more weedy. Littlestone tunnels had always been wet and when, in 1936, the pump draining them showed signs of giving up it was not thought worth the expense of replacing it. Instead the trackbed was raised, reducing the loading gauge from 6ft 7in to 5ft 9in and the Clayton Pullmans were cut down to suit; fortunately the new saloons were already within the new loading gauge and the few remaining articulated sets were simply restricted to providing short workings on the New Romney–Hythe section.

FAILURE OF HURRICANE

During this time, the Captain was certainly not apathetic about generating traffic. The 1936 high-season timetable, for example, required no less than six locomotives in service as the roster below shows.

RH & DR Locomotive Diagrams: August 1936

Diagram 1			Diagram 2		
arr		dep	arr		dep
	Littlestone	9.30		Littlestone	9.30
10.00	Hythe	10.30	9.50	Dungeness	9.50
11.30	Dungeness	12.00	10.40	Hythe	11.00
1.00	Hythe	2.00	11.50	Dungeness	12.45
2.50	Dungeness	ECS	1.40	Hythe	2.45
ECS	Littlestone	3.30	3.35	Dungeness	4.30
4.00	Hythe	4.30	5.20	Hythe	6.00
5.20	Dungeness	6.15	7.00	Dungeness	7.30
7.05	Hythe	7.30	8.00	Littlestone	
8.00	Littlestone				

Diagram 4			Diagram 5		
arr		dep	arr		dep
	Littlestone	10.30		Littlestone	12.10
10.50	Dungeness	10.50	12.45	Hythe	1.00
11.40	Hythe	12.00	1.50	Dungeness	1.50
12.30	Littlestone	3.10	2.40	Hythe	3.15
3.40	Hythe	4.00	4.05	Dungeness	4.10
4.15	Dymchurch	4.40	4.30	Littlestone	4.45
4.55	Hythe	5.15	5.05	Dungeness	5.05
5.45	Littlestone	6.00	5.25	Littlestone	6.15
6.30	Hythe	6.45	6.35	Dungeness	6.35
7.15	Littlestone	8.00	6.55	Littlestone	
8.30	Hythe	9.00			
9.30	Littlestone				

Diagram 6 (Relief)			Diagram 3 (When required)		
arr		dep	arr		dep
	Littlestone	3.00		Littlestone	10.35
3.20	Dungeness	3.20	11.55	Hythe	
3.40	Littlestone	4.00	Dymchurch shuttles as required		
4.30	Hythe		5.45	Hythe	6.25
			6.55	Littlestone	

Since this roster left only one or two locomotives spare there were no doubt a few crises, especially since a succession of small failures culminated occasionally in a grand one; for example in July 1937, *Hurricane*, the Captain's personal engine and the last three-cylinder one, failed somewhat dramatically en route to Hythe with the 4.20pm train, disorganising traffic for the rest of the day. It may be worthwhile clearing up this event since there are many rumours about it. What happened was that the previous day Howey had complained that the engine had an irregular beat. Mr A. A. Binfield, then working with H. C. S. Bullock at Farnborough, happened to be in New Romney, examined the engine and found defects in the inside motion. Howey was advised not to run the locomotive in that condition but for some reason did so, and the result was that in service the valve gear partially disintegrated, the whole thing locking solid in a tangle of flailing rods. The cylinder did not seize, nor was the steam chest affected but the locomotive was brought to a sudden stand and could not be moved until the jammed motion had been disconnected. A man from Paxman's then spent the best part of a week poking around with little success until Howey, impatient, decided to rebuild the locomotive as a two-cylinder one. By a fortunate coincidence *Southern Maid*'s wheels had just been returned and were standing in the shed. Mr Binfield returned to New Romney for a week and with some help rebuilt *Hurricane* on these wheels which she still retains. The centre motion was removed, the cylinder, steam chest and steam connections being blanked off.

It is only fair to say that constant problems had been experienced with the three-cylinder machines. They were very heavy consumers of coal and water, tended to be slower in accelerating and were in general less popular with the men. *Typhoon* had been converted to two-cylinder by Davey Paxman's in 1935 and *Hurricane* was only retained because she was Captain Howey's favourite.

BALLAST TRAFFIC

A desire to generate traffic was also responsible for the restoration to working order of *Hercules* during winter 1936–7. There was a local demand for shingle ballast and Captain Howey decided to take advantage of it. Six ex-Ravenglass hopper wagons were refurbished with side-doors in place of their former bottom discharge doors and a siding was laid in between Maddieson's and the WD siding to 'tap' a bank of shingle that was available there. It was connected to the up-main by a pair of padlocked points and was from time to time moved fanwise by platelayers to allow new areas of beach to be exploited (it should be explained that 'beach' is the local term for shingle).

Normal procedure was for the six hoppers to be loaded during the day by a gang of itinerant labourers. They were then picked up the following morning by *Hercules*, sent light engine from New Romney, and taken to Hythe where an elevated ramp had been erected. At first a rather dangerous procedure was adopted whereby the wagons where placed in the station and the locomotive retired with one at a time onto the 'down' main line. The locomotive accelerated into the siding, pushing its lone hopper as far up the ramp as it could before it was brought to a standstill. At this point, usually about two-thirds of the way up, sprags were hastily thrust between the wagon wheels and the side doors were opened to let the ballast cascade down. The dangers of this method were obvious and as soon as a gravity fed hopper had been completed at the ramp top a winch was bought so that the wagons could be hauled up the slope. Sadly the venture did not prosper since most customers wanted crushed ballast which the railway could not supply; it appears that the traffic only ran during some months of 1937 and was then discontinued: certainly during the high season it was somewhat inconvenient, involving a 5.30am working into Hythe and a return trip before the normal passenger workings began.

Some ballast may also have been taken from a cutting between Lade and The Pilot since in 1937 the line here was lowered. This was mainly because uncontrolled housing development had resulted in several blind level crossings two of which were replaced by over-bridges, the line apparently being moved bodily into the cutting once it was dug out. The bridges, rather oddly, had no parapets at first, these not being added until after the war.

At about the same time a long siding was put in at Dungeness, leading off to weigh-houses by a standard gauge spur but this was apparently nothing to do with ballast. The Southern had closed its Dungeness branch to passengers in 1937 and it seems the RH & D hoped again to capture some of the fish traffic. There is no evidence that this ever reached substantial proportions.

The closing of the SR's Dungeness branch was caused partly by that company's realisation that the Romney had a very lucrative

summer traffic from the new development around Lade and
Greatstone. The SR therefore rerouted its New Romney line part
way down the Dungeness section and then round in a big loop to
run parallel for some miles with the RH & D's Dungeness extension.
There is a rather shakily authenticated story about this that may
nonetheless bear repeating. Captain Howey was always feuding with
the SR over the eligibility of his staff for railwayman's privilege
tickets. He was just smarting from his latest rebuff, or so the story
goes, when the SR's legal department put in a routine request for the
new route to cross his WD siding on the level. The Southern was
so confident that formation and sleepers were already being laid
when a crisp reply pointed out that the line was WD property and
the War Department, on the advice of its local technical adviser, felt
that interference with its right of way might be detrimental to the
country's defence . . . who was the adviser? None other than Captain
J. E. P. Howey! Whatever the rights or wrongs of the case, the WD
siding was clearly regarded as a railway in being and the Southern
branch was carried over it on a short girder bridge. Site evidence
suggests that the narrow gauge was lowered several feet to avoid too
much of a 'hump' for the standard gauge.

The two major events of 1938 were the retirement of Bob Hardie
from his joint post of traffic manager and Hythe station master, and
the inauguration of a special express service, The Blue Train. For
this a set of ten Hythe saloons and a van were painted a medium
('Caledonian') blue and *Hurricane* was painted to match, her name
for some reason being changed to *Bluebottle*. Apart from the colour
it is difficult to see why so inappropriate a name was chosen unless
perhaps it was a 'miniatureised' take-off of the LNER's A4s named
after birds. In 1938, there was also a further outbreak of miniatures
on the line when a short 10¼in gauge railway was laid on the down
side at Dymchurch; it used a locomotive and equipment acquired from
the estate of the late H. C. S. Bullock of Farnborough who, it appears,
had been commissioned to produce a 15in gauge Stanier 4–6–2 but
had not done much work on it before his untimely death.

HOWEY AND HIS FRIENDS

The pre-war years were thus a fairly placid period on the whole
but it seems appropriate to mention here one very unusual feature
peculiar to the 15in gauge—the R & ER also suffered from it to a

limited extent in its early formative years. We have seen that the railway was regarded locally as something of a private plaything for the Captain and in many ways this was true. Certainly one of his favourite ploys was to invite friends down during the summer to 'play with the railway'—in particular to try their hand at engine driving. A very colourful crowd they must have been from all accounts, including both the Holder cousins, well known in 15in gauge circles, Mr Bramwell the locomotive superintendent at Liverpool Street LNER and his two nephews who were LNER men, Mr Dan Crittall of Crittalls Metal Windows fame and a Mr Goddard who was universally known as 'Jumbo'. It must be recorded that even if they were amateurs, as enginemen they were expected to behave strictly in accordance with both the letter and the spirit of the law, working their full turns alongside the regular men. Captain Howey had a reputation even then of being very strict about such things. He had no compunction about dismissing permanent staff whom he felt were not upholding the standards he demanded and he is said to have applied just the same standards to his friends. Given those conditions they were no doubt a very useful source of the seasonal labour required by the greatly augmented summer service.

To one who never knew Captain Howey personally, the impression given by those who knew him is that he was autocratic and aloof but at the same time rather a shy man in some ways. He may not have paid very high salaries but he did keep a considerable number in employment during difficult times and went to some trouble to provide amenities for them. The railway even built two blocks of six cottages in Station Road for its workers and one of the first building additions when the railway was complete was a social club over the carriage shed which was available to all the railway personnel. Old employees recall the Captain as having a liking for both amateur and professional dramatics and as being an accomplished performer on the accordion. He was wont to invite leading local artists to perform at the social club and, if he liked a particular show at a local theatre, would sometimes make a block booking for his staff on Saturday nights, taking over the running of the evening passenger service himself so that everyone could be free to go.

CHAPTER 5

The War and After

WINTER 1939

The outbreak of the war found the RH & D nearing the end of a very intensive high season timetable. The initial impact of wartime came almost at once since mobilisation plans were immediately in force and holiday camps along the Dungeness peninsular were promptly taken over as reservist training camps. Among them was the Duke of York's camp at St Mary's Bay allocated to the territorial battalion of the Artists' Rifles. A more or less chance meeting between their officers and Captain Howey on 3 December led the latter to make a typically sporting gesture: to help in transporting the battalion from Sandling to St Mary's Bay he was prepared to cancel all regular trains on the following Tuesday and run troop trains instead. Contemporary accounts suggest that a single train of no less than sixty vehicles was made up, powered by three locomotives in front and two at the rear and that this made two trips during the afternoon.

Apart from this isolated incident, however, the outbreak of war did not at first have much lasting effect on the RH & D. It was in any case nearing the end of the season and it would appear that the normal winter timetable was simply started earlier than usual. The winter service proved useful to the local inhabitants under wartime conditions and it was certainly continued into 1940—there are tickets and timetables of that period extant. It has not proved possible to determine exactly when services were terminated but it was almost certainly before 22 May 1940, the date on which National Emergency Powers were taken to evacuate civilian personnel from danger areas. The majority of the civilian population was quickly evacuated from the Dungeness peninsular since with the rapid German advance into France during May and early June, the area was an obvious target for any invasion. Following the series of military setbacks culminating in the Dunkirk evacuation of British forces, the whole Kent coast was declared an invasion zone and put under military control. Static defences mushroomed and various units moved in to take up positions in what was in effect the British front line.

THE ARMY TAKES OVER

Among them was the 6th Battalion, the Somerset Light Infantry, commanded by Colonel D. I. L. Beath, which had moved into the area prepatory to going to France and which now took over the sector beween Hythe and New Romney. It must be remembered that, with the withdrawal from France, the meagre British army had lost most of its transport and its lack could not nearly be made up by requisitioning civilian vehicles; in any case petrol was short. The presence of the RH & D forming a natural line of communication along the battalion's front must therefore have appeared something of a godsend to the military defenders of that area and Colonel Beath took some fairly rapid action. An investigation convinced him that he had in the battalion two shunting drivers, two firemen and enough ex-railwaymen of other grades to make up a railway detachment. An approach was therefore made to the division controlling the area and the railway was formally requisitioned (taken over for military use) on 15 June 1940.

The section between New Romney and Hythe in particular was immediately put into use as battalion transport, carrying leave parties to and from Hythe, collecting new troops off main line trains and performing such essential domestic journeys as conveying the laundry. To provide it with at least a small element of mobile firepower, the battalion officers thought up the idea of an armoured train and Woolwich Arsenal and the Southern Railway's Ashford Works converted the idea into reality. This emerged in the summer of 1940 as a 'three car unit', with No 5 *Hercules* sandwiched between two of the ex-R & ER bogie hopper wagons. All were clad in mild steel boiler plate to provide some protection against small-arms fire and the wagons additionally had concrete screening at vital points. Each wagon was fitted with two Lewis light machine guns and a Boys anti-tank rifle—not a particularly effective weapon, but all that was available. The battalion's headquarters was at Dymchurch and for the first few weeks the train was kept in a siding there, with steam up at all times. As German air activity intensified, it was decided that the train would have to be concealed and the corps intelligence officer, Captain Oliver Messel, had a fake 'hill' constructed over a specially laid siding about three quarters of a mile east of Dymchurch station; the location cannot now be traced with certainty but the most likely patch of land is at Burmarsh Road. If this was so it might well explain the vague indications that a siding once existed at that station. During this period the line was visited by such notables as Sir (then Mr) Winston Churchill and the Duke of Gloucester, both of whom duly admired the train—or so it is said. It appears that, despite the odd lurid painting, the train was never seriously used in action although its crew always claimed they had destroyed at least one enemy aircraft. The railway detachment *did* shoot down a German fighter at New Romney but this act was performed by a corporal balancing his Lewis gun on the shoulder of another man.

USE BY THE ROYAL ENGINEERS

As everyone knows, the threatened invasion never took place, and at the end of October 1940 the Somersets were relieved by the 4th Battalion Royal West Kents who did not have the same interest in the line. They would appear to have used it spasmodically but not with the same degree of skill and when the Royal Engineers finally assumed control in 1941 it was in a rather sad state with various locomotives completely unserviceable. Mr A. A. Binfield recalls being asked on several occasions to go down to New Romney and advise the RE unit on how to sort matters out.

The Royal Engineers had a substantial body of troops in the peninsular for the remainder of the war and the railway itself was operated by an RE Railway Company—or a detachment thereof— until it was derequisitioned in 1945. For several years it was used both for recreational transport and as a training railway for RE staff. As early as spring 1942, preparations for the subsequent allied invasion of Europe were already under way and the area between Hythe and Dungeness was ideal for troop training; not only did it have vast stretches of deserted beach but the former holiday camps provided excellent accommodation for large bodies of men. Hence the railway ran a regular service of trains between Hythe and Dungeness with roughly hourly departures from each end during the afternoon and evening. A special late evening train from Hythe was put on at weekends for those returning from leave or from a night out on the town. Few records of the period are available but a visitor in May 1942 recorded the railway as being fairly active with some six locomotives in use and two regular trainsets, one of six and one of seven coaches. Of the locomotives completely out of use *Samson* was, of course, still derelict while No 10 was semi-dismantled in a shed following derailment in a bomb crater. The line appeared to be in good condition and the operating staff were even bothering to repaint equipment when needed.

THE PLUTO OPERATION

This state of affairs might well have continued until the war's end but the area was chosen to play a part in the allied invasion plans. The major problem about landing in Normandy was that all supplies would have to be transported to the front along ever lengthening lines of communication until a major port was captured—and the Germans would hold onto major ports very tenaciously.

This problem had been anticipated to some extent and in particular the problem of oil fuel supply had been examined carefully. The result of the deliberations was PLUTO—Pipeline Under The Ocean; this was in essence a series of highly flexible three-inch pipelines that were to be laid from the Dungeness coast to a point near Boulogne, with pumping stations on both sides. The pipes themselves came ready wound on 70ft diameter floating drums known as Conundrums, and they were laid in the same manner as undersea cables. Much equipment was, however, needed at the landward end together with various runs of pipe to connect storage tanks and pumping stations and the railway played a part in providing this.

The pipeline head was situated near Lade, a number of the holiday bungalows in the area being completely gutted so that the storage tanks and pumps could be installed under 'natural' camouflage. Much equipment and piping was brought in via New Romney and the station was temporarily converted into welding shops, the overall roof over the through lines providing a convenient 'shed' in which work could be done. The blast walls erected here and at Dymchurch along the sides of the overall roof structures during 1940, proved very useful as windbreaks! Very little other alteration took place except that a 15in gauge line was laid in down the middle of the railway's standard gauge siding to facilitate trans-shipment of lengths of pipe.

These were welded up in the station to lengths of approximately 300ft and were then conveyed over the railway to the pumping site. Again details are scarce but it appears that a motley collection of underframes was marshalled into a single 'train' which included the remaining articulated frames (probably three quint-sets), a number of four-wheeled flats and even some 16ft Hudson bogie frames. The drag of the pipe must have caused considerable disturbance to the track and there is some evidence that, in the later stages at least, bulldozers were used to drag the bundles of pipes over the final section. Certainly by early 1945, when all the excitement had died down, the railway was not in regular use beyond Greatstone and the track was extensively damaged between Maddieson's Camp and a point just short of Lade. Beyond Lade it was entirely disused and had suffered the sort of damage that disused track is usually subject to!

It is fairly clear that from mid-1944 on the railway became somewhat neglected owing to pressure of other work on the part of the Royal Engineers. Some sort of service was maintained between New Romney and Hythe right up to the summer of 1945 but maintenance was undoubtedly slackened and by July of that year, when the line was finally de-requisitioned, its condition left a great deal to be desired. Certainly Captain Howey thought so when he once more took over control.

REHABILITATION

A quick survey showed that the greater part of the Dungeness line was completely unusable, and that a great deal of work would be necessary both on stock and track before a public passenger service could be restored even between New Romney and Hythe. Accordingly a claim for compensation was entered against the War Office and the Captain was forced to accept that no real progress would be possible until the 1946 season. To provide some revenue and to cater for what summer visitors there were in 1945, the down line was regauged to 10¼in between New Romney engine sheds and The Warren bridge. It appears this was done simply by relocating one rail and the ex-Bullock 0–6–0PT and stock from the former 10¼in line at Dymchurch were used to provide a shuttle service during August and September. No timetables were issued, the train running very much on the 'any more for the *Skylark*' principle.

With the end of the summer 'service', work started in earnest to patch up the railway. In October Major J. T. Holder, son of one of the original directors, was appointed general manager and a five-year restoration plan was worked out. As an immediate measure, a large quantity of ex-WD sleepers (unused) was acquired from a depot at Newcastle and a gang of German prisoners-of-war was loaned to the company to provide labour for refettling the line between New Romney and Hythe. Having been in use for most of the war this was in fair order but required a great deal of weeding and the replacement of many sleepers. Hythe station was cleaned up and the roof repaired while the signalling was brought back to pre-war standard. Lurid tales of smashed interlocking date from this period but it appears that these were somewhat exaggerated; the interlocks were disconnected rather than smashed though a few of the link pins may have been sheared through application of brute force. Meanwhile, the various items of rolling stock scattered around the line were collected, the best being overhauled while the rest were put aside for future repair or rebuilding; arrangements were made with the Southern Railway to rebuild some locomotives at their Ashford works, others were overhauled at New Romney.

In consequence of much hard work during winter 1945–6, it proved possible to open for public service on 1 March 1946. The inaugural train was sent off by the mayor of New Romney who rode on it to Hythe where he was greeted by the mayor of that town. The train was pulled by No 8, renamed *Hurricane* for the opening, and after the usual junketings a restricted service was operated during the spring and early summer. By 1 August, when the high season time-table came into operation, it had proved possible to extend services to the re-opened Maddieson's Holiday Camp and no less than eleven return trips daily were advertised between Hythe and New Romney, with two additional late evening workings on Saturdays only. Most trains to Maddieson's only ran past New Romney if required.

MORE BALLAST

Meanwhile, various other events were taking place. After a close inspection of the derelict Dungeness extension, Captain Howey had decided to rebuild it as single line only. Money was tight at that time and he did not feel the cost of maintaining a double road would be justified; moreover he realised that by cannibalising the worst damaged line—that on the landward side—it would be possible to restore a single track without buying in any new material. Work was therefore pressed forward during 1946 and the early part of 1947, ballast being obtained from pits near the old Sonar reflectors. To provide extra revenue, a new company, the Romney Marsh Ballast Co, was formed in 1946 by some of the RH & D directors and several local businessmen to exploit these pits. A crusher was erected on the site and the railway resuscitated its ballast ramp and hoppers at Hythe station. In addition to the five remaining bogie hopper wagons, sixty tipping wagons were acquired, the railway providing chassis from its derelict stock while the ballast company supplied the skip bodies. To provide power *Hercules* was overhauled at Ashford and—wonder of wonders—the remains of *Samson* were collected together and sent off to Clifford Edwards Ltd of Hove for a complete rebuild. The ballast trains were intended to work all the year round and in summer this involved workings early in the morning and late at night to avoid disturbing the passenger service. Trains loaded to thirty unbraked skips were normal and a number of staff testify that working such trains was no sinecure, especially when the shingle was wet and the rails slippery. The WD siding rose steeply to its junction with the main line, necessitating a full-throttle charge to avoid stalling, while on down-grades the unbraked deadweight often threatened to take control of the locomotive. In winter, too, the shingle was quite likely to freeze in the trucks so that it was not unknown for the whole thing to overbalance when being tipped on the ramp at Hythe. Great hopes were placed on this traffic but, as we shall see, it never came up to expectation.

Nor, alas, did various other projects of the period. In 1946 serious consideration was given to extending along the canal into Hythe town centre and the route was even surveyed . . . but a bus-service rendered it unnecessary. The East Kent Road Car Co agreed to extend its service 103 to Hythe (RH & D) Station, thus saving the railway money and providing free publicity at one stroke for all buses bore the legend 'Light Railway Station' on their destination blinds. About the same time, too, Mr Holcroft, formerly of the Great Western Railway and the Southern Railway, was commissioned to design a fast mixed-traffic 2–8–2 for the RH & D, the first of an increasingly complex series of railway projects that included American-style 2–8–4s and even Duplexii. None of them were built, although the 2–8–2 certainly reached the stage of a fully worked out design, and it seems likely that the failure of the ballast working made them redundant.

In early 1947, however, this was not clear. Indeed the railway was expecting a considerable increase in traffic for further four-wheeled underframes were ordered from Clifford Edwards to act as skip chassis while a steady programme of coach rebuilding went on. Mainstay of the programme were various 16ft-chassis of the 1934–5 batch from which the Army had stripped their bodies, or which had been damaged by enemy action. Eventually a total of fifteen open coaches was built, of which about eight were available for the 1947 season; to celebrate the expected restoration of the Dungeness service and the reintroduction of the Bluecoaster two observation cars, *Pluto* and *Martello* were built on similar chassis, and a set of Hythe saloons was overhauled; fortunately the Army had been very fond of blue paint so they were already in the right livery!

Theoretically the railway was still running a Saturdays-only winter timetable of nine trains daily each way with four extended to Maddieson's 'if required' but it was certainly suspended for at least some weeks during the winter to allow total occupation of the track for maintenance purposes.

Encouragingly, work was far enough advanced to allow a formal re-opening of the Dungeness section on 21 March 1947. At the time, there were still considerable relics of the military occupation lying around and Dungeness itself was entirely cut off by barbed wire entanglements through which a hole had been cut for the railway. Mr G. A. Barlow clearly recollects being sent off with one of the, then new, observation cars to carry out clearance trials and being threatened with dire penalties if he came back with so much as a scratch on it. Fortunately all went well and the still immaculate car was able to be used at the grand opening, by film comedians Laurel and Hardy, no less. Full services to the lighthouse were resumed from Easter 1947 and conditions got better and better as the debris of military occupation was slowly cleared away: even the villas previously gutted to contain PLUTO installations were restored again and, with petrol and cars still almost unobtainable, holiday traffic soared. It was common practice to have to run trains in two or three portions and the shortage of stock became an acute embarrassment. As a somewhat desperate measure Captain Howey even purchased the complete Eaton Railway, thus providing three more passenger vehicles and a horde of rather useless trucks. Even luggage wagons were used on peak days and as a final resort the sole remaining articulated set was brought out of retirement and fitted with open bodywork.

Even so it was clear that more would be needed and Howey's eye fell on the surviving ballast hopper wagons. With sixty skips in use these were largely superfluous and so in spring 1947 they were stripped of their bodies and new coach bodies were ordered for the chassis; meanwhile rebuilding of ex-16ft saloons continued and the Rolls was rebuilt with new bodywork to provide an extra motive power unit. It was fitted with a Fordson engine two years later.

Conditions at the time were somewhat primitive for the hard pressed staff, almost every available suitable building being pressed into use for accommodation purposes; they included, besides the bungalows or houses at Dymchurch and Dungeness, such undesirable residences as The Pilot station—used even before the war—and the rooms comprising the present company offices. George Barlow lived at The Pilot for a few months before moving to the latter, a feat he performed after work one night by using the *Goddess* and a collection of wagons and coaches as a furniture train.

The year 1948 saw continued improvement in passenger services and stock; the ex-hopper wagons were fitted with smart but flimsy bodies in Pullman colours and the train of five was ready for the summer season; Mr Hooper, the railway's very competent carpenter, carried on rebuilding former saloons, in both closed and open form, and also produced four very wide-bodied open coaches on Clifford Edwards chassis; for the first time in many years the railway had all nine steam locomotives available for traffic since *Samson* was back from her rebuild. In consequence a more intensive high season service was possible and speeds were almost at pre-war levels.

An epic event of the 1948 season was, perhaps, the second longest train the railway had ever run. The Annual Branch Delegates Conference of the National Union of Railwaymen was held locally that year and in May the railway put on a special train for the delegates. Composed of no fewer than 47 coaches it was hauled by *Green Goddess, Typhoon* and *Hurricane* and must have created something of an operating problem. Suitable refreshment stops were made at Lade and Dungeness after which the train returned at speed to Hythe. There a smooth operation was carried out whereby the train came to a halt outside the station, the two leading engines uncoupled and ran forward while the third engine pulled into Hythe station with the front third of the train. A second engine then backed down and collected the next portion after which the third engine brought

Page 71 (above) *The site of the turning wye at The Pilot, photographed from the air in 1972. The trackbed is clearly visible;* (below) *Dungeness station about 1930. The wind pump can be clearly seen – as can the sagging signals and weatherbeaten fence*

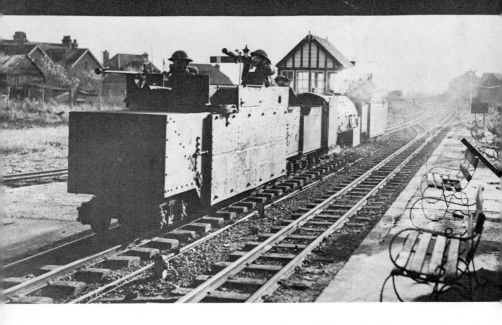

Page 72 (above) *The armoured train running through Dymchurch, apparently on the wrong line! The Boys anti-tank rifle with its associated Lewis gun is at the front end of the truck while an AA Lewis gun is mounted behind. The short-lived 10¼in gauge line can be seen behind the train; (below) A 1958 view of New Romney, showing (in train) the 1935 saloons and a Hooper (1956) rebuild; (in siding) a 'Queen Anne' with brake compartment and one without*

in the remainder. A beautifully smooth operation in most respects though it was, one gigantic flaw in the organisation now appeared. While the locomotives after their extended run may have been low on water, the convivial passengers after their extended refreshment stops were in just the opposite condition and Hythe station toilets could cope with only five at a time—for a short period the railway's public relations must have been seriously strained.

If passenger traffic was booming, however, the ballast traffic to Hythe had proved to be short-lived. Some operational problems had arisen in any case—for one whole winter *Samson* had to work coupled to *Hurricane*'s tender to provide an adequate water supply; all the skip bodies had to have holes drilled in them so that water would escape and not freeze; some of the skips had proved unsuitable and there was at least one spectacular derailment, at St Mary's Bay, when shingle and vehicles were strewn lavishly across both tracks. In addition the ballast company found the long haul inconvenient and un-economical, so the hoppers were moved to New Romney. An inclined siding was put in along the rear of the down-side carriage shed and the winch from Hythe was installed. Even this arrangement did not last for more than a few months, however, for the company then took the logical step of moving its crusher complete to a field near the line at New Romney. A steep siding, facing to Dungeness, was put in near Church Lane Crossing and the ballast company was granted running powers over the RH & D main line thence to WD siding. It took over the ex-Eaton Railway Simplex tractor and from early 1949 up to about 1951 worked its own trains of uncrushed ballast at times when no passenger service was running. In March 1951 the concern went over to road transport and ballast traffic on the RH & DR finally ceased. The ramps and hoppers were dismantled, the skips divided between railway and ballast company, and the Simplex was returned to the RH & D.

Yet this is anticipating events a little for several things had happened to the railway by then. Major Holder left at the end of the 1948 season and was replaced by Colonel R. B. Y. Simpson. The remains of the Dungeness 'up' road were lifted piecemeal from 1949 onward, providing a valuable reserve of track material that lasted until 1970. The Dymchurch shuttles were discontinued at the end of the 1948 season, all short workings from then on running to and from New Romney (see chapter eleven), and the 1949 timetable actually required seven locomotives in steam daily—a feature that

E

continued until 1962. Hythe shed was used for locomotive purposes for several years in the 1950s.

A QUIET TIME

From 1949 until the Captain's death in 1963, however, there was comparatively little excitement. These years were ones of consolidation and with one big exception the 'memorable' events were comparatively trivial ones so far as the general running of the line was concerned. In 1950, the Captain bought a small standard gauge 0-4-4T *Dunrobin* from the Duke of Sutherland's private railway, together with a saloon coach. Railway No 3 was extended a hundred yards or so back onto RH & D property, a small shed was built and the two acquisitions retired within it, appearing in steam only on high days and holidays when they trundled solemnly up to the level crossing and back. Various minor alterations to buildings took place. Between 1953 and 1955 Bob Hobbs, a driver, performed what can only be called a labour of love in numbering and classifying all the stock; from all accounts he got precious little encouragement or thanks for his pains! In 1954 there was a notable accident when a newly built four-wheeled brake van was blown over by the wind on Half-Mile Curve; in its turn it overturned the tender of *Hercules*, which had by some error been built far too high at Ashford, and that overbalanced the locomotive. The whole lot finished up on their sides and some cutting-down and modification ensued! There were several other accidents at various times from the usual causes—unwary road vehicles being hit on level crossings or, once or twice, enginemen being knocked unconscious on the low bridges. Once in 1967 *Hercules* overran the the buffers at Hythe and finished up in the forecourt but there was nothing quite so sensational as that pre-war occasion when *Doctor Syn* broke away from her tender on the Dungeness road—the guard couldn't at first work out why the train was slowing while the engine beats got faster but others could . . . the driver sitting disconsolately in his tender, had to watch his engine disappearing rapidly in the distance under full steam and quite a number of others got the shock of their lives as the driverless *Doctor Syn* rocketed past them. She got right to the Dungeness loop before derailing on the long curve and ending up on her side.

Other minor events were also concerned with engines: the RH & D has quite a tradition now of visiting locomotives but it started only in the late 1950s. In 1959 one of the Carron Company 4–4–2s from Sutton Coldfield was completed by T. Hunt and came down for a while. *Sutton Flyer* looked tiny against the 1:3 scale Pacifics as did an experimental diesel-hydraulic *Royal Anchor* which came on trial at her owner's request in 1957. Designed and built by Charles Lane of Liphook, *Royal Anchor* also was not a great success since she consumed more power in the transmission process than ever reached the rail wheels so after lying at Hythe for some time she was returned to her owner's executors; she was later purchased by the Ravenglass & Eskdale.

Some indication of the even tenor of the line's existence can be judged from the fact that after Colonel Simpson left in September 1952 no new manager was appointed. Foreman Driver Barlow virtually ran the operating side right up to 1961 when Peter Catt was promoted from driver to general superintendent and George Barlow officially became locomotive superintendent. The minimum of money was spent on general maintenance and Captain Howey's policy appeared to be one of 'let it run'; indeed more than once he is said to have indicated that he would be quite happy as long as it 'saw him out'. Notwithstanding this relaxed policy, however, the Captain still maintained his usual sharp eye for detail. It was no uncommon thing for a driver whose concentration had slipped slightly to be greeted on return by a sharp question as to why he had or had not done such and such a thing—'the old man' from all accounts had and uncanny knack of being around in the right place at the wrong time! It must also be recorded much to Captain Howey's credit that even if he was reluctant to spend money on the small but essential everyday things he did make one large expenditure without which the railway would not be running today. Following experiments with proper superheating on *Northern Chief* in 1952, he decided to equip all nine locomotives with new superheated standard boilers at a cost of something like £1,000 apiece. The work was started in 1956 and all but No 10 were reboilered before the Captain's death in 1963. No 10's boiler had been delivered but was not fitted until the following year.

Yet, if the 1950s were uneventful from the organisational point of view, one social event must be recorded. On 30 March 1957, the railway was honoured by a visit from Her Majesty the Queen, the Duke of Edinburgh, Prince Charles and Princess Anne. The up line was under repair at the time and since they wished to travel from New Romney to Hythe a special train was run on the down line. It was headed by No 8 *Hurricane* in charge of Foreman Driver Barlow, the Duke and the royal children taking it in turns to travel on the footplate.

CAPTAIN HOWEY DIES

This notwithstanding, it is probably true to say that up till 1963 the railway was in a gentle decline. Renewals in stock did not really keep pace with wastage and there was little motive power to spare. At Whitsun 1963 there was, indeed, a fairly serious accident at Palmarsh when a down shuttle train, which should not have been in section, ran into the back of a Dungeness working, stalled for lack of steam. There were no fatalities but with No 10 already unserviceable the resulting damage to locomotives and stock forced the abandonment of the high season timetable for that year—though oddly enough there was little drop in revenue. On 8 September Captain Howey, by then an old man of almost 77, died and the whole future of the railway was put in doubt. It ran until the end of the normal season and then closed down for the winter.

CHAPTER 6

Modern Times

MR COLLINS BUYS A RAILWAY

With Captain Howey's death the future of the railway was for the first time in the balance. The Captain had always indicated tacitly that he was not much concerned with what happened after his death and had made no definite provision. His widow, Mrs G. M. Howey, took over the running of the company, to which she had in any case been secretary for a number of years, but she did not feel able to continue indefinitely. After some negotiations, therefore, the whole railway was sold in July 1964 to a Mr S. H. Collins and his partner Mr J. E. Scatcherd. These two, retired bankers, took over on 1 July, acquiring in all some 49,000 of the original 51,000 shares. Mr Collins also bought Red Tiles, the Howeys' bungalow.

Mr Collins became managing director, Peter Catt was appointed general manager and George Barlow became locomotive superintendent and, in 1968, operating manager. Otherwise the railway continued much as before although attempts were made to increase its commercial viability. In particular a quite extensive café was erected beside *Modelland* over the downside carriage shed, providing adequate catering facilities for the first time; New Romney station was slightly improved by extending the up plaform back towards Littlestone Road bridge and by resiting the footbridge in its present position; and a start was made on catching up on arrears of maintenance. In 1966 the Railway Company even declared a dividend on the ordinary shares of four per cent—for the first time in its life, and similar dividends were paid for the next four years. Unfortunately not much had been done when Peter Catt died suddenly in March 1968 and Mr Collins decided that he no longer wished to carry on. The railway at that moment in time was in a state of some difficulty since not only did it no longer have a general manager but there was a gaping hole in its track; the Duke of York's Bridge had finally succumbed to forty-odd years of wear and tear and was in course of replacement. It was only by unremitting work on the part of all staff that the new bridge was installed and track relaid just one day before the first special of the year was due to run.

. . . AND SELLS IT

Once more the future appeared somewhat uncertain but fortunately buyers were soon found. A consortium of local businessmen headed by Messrs D. B. Lye and A. Record agreed to take over the company and also to buy Red Tiles, Mr Collins remaining on the board until a loan debt was repaid. The new owners took over on 20 May 1968, installing Mr P. C. Hawkins as their general manager. Mr Lye himself became chairman and Mr Record the managing director. The new owners, businessmen rather than railwaymen, found in their turn that they had inherited a good many problems. They initiated a number of projects, in particular the development of a modern machine shop at New Romney, and granted a substantial increase in wages for the staff. They had agreed to finance the rebuilding of Collins (née Duke of York's) Bridge but were rather shaken to find that this was not an isolated case; no less than four other underline bridges required total renewal and their condition was symptomatic of the whole condition of the railway. It very soon became obvious that very heavy capital expenditure would be needed if the railway was to be a viable proposition, since many items were coming to the end of their useful life. This expenditure the new syndicate was not prepared to undertake, although it did sanction the purchase of a quantity of ex-Sierra Leone Government Railways 30lb rail; indeed it might well have had difficulty in finding the money for such a venture.

DESPERATE STRAITS

The syndicate then (summer 1969) started to examine possible ways of saving the situation without having entirely to close the railway. It had for some years been clear that as tourist railways go the RH & D was uneconomically long in comparison with the fares that could be charged and during 1969 and 1970 several plans were proposed to shorten the length of run and to capitalise on some of the assets—in particular the valuable land sites at Hythe and New Romney. The first serious scheme was to run only from Hythe to Dymchurch, a new terminal station and depot being proposed at the latter place. The derelict Silver Waves holiday camp was even purchased to provide a site near the sea front but the council would not allow a vital road crossing. Another idea was to run only as far as Burmarsh Road, the suggestion being that a field would be bought at Burmarsh to allow a big return loop to be laid in while a much reduced but very high quality fleet of locomotives and coaches would be stabled at Hythe. Yet another idea, quite seriously mooted, was to give up the Hythe section entirely and to run only the Dungeness extension, an idea which would have had the advantage of retaining existing facilities at New Romney. All these plans would have allowed the company to sell at least some of the land it owned and to cut down both its staff and its rolling stock; a final stock of three or four locomotives and some 30 high quality coaches was envisaged.

Fortunately none of these schemes came to fruition. The nearest any idea came to being put into practice was when the owners of the former Duke of York's Camp at Jesson, now the Schools Journey Centre, almost purchased the railway early in 1971. Their plan would have involved running from Hythe to St Mary's Bay with a new terminus in a former turkey farm there, but the SJC board decided by a narrow majority not to acquire the line.

The controlling syndicate appears to have become somewhat disheartened and, since it could not agree on the course of action required, had perforce to do almost nothing. To its credit it completed the replacement of all five shaky bridges but no major expenditure was sanctioned thereafter and by Christmas 1970 spending had virtually ceased. Henceforward the railway reverted to a policy of minimum maintenance and talk of possible total closure began to be heard.

THE CONSORTIUM

Yet again, for the third time in six years, the railway appeared to be facing disaster—a striking contrast to the previous 40 uneventful years and, in a way, a testimony to the extent to which it had depended on one man—Captain Howey—to keep it going. This time, however, the railway's staff themselves were getting very worried and G. A. Barlow alerted a number of fairly wealthy enthusiasts as to what was happening. The result was that a consortium was formed in the spring of 1971, under the leadership of Messrs W. A. McAlpine, R. A. North and J. B. Hollingsworth, to investigate the possibility of buying the line. Matters were brought to a head because the operating surplus was decreasing year by year and a small loss was forecast for 1972.

The owning syndicate themselves decided that some drastic action was needed. Mr Lye bought out his major partner Mr A. Record, and, along with his fellow directors, decided that the railway should be closed unless any enthusiast consortium could rescue it within a short time. This decision was announced at the company's annual general meeting on 28 August 1971 and the staff were warned that closure was very likely; indeed redundancy procedures were actually initiated. In retrospect this decision, while intensely disturbing for the staff whose livelihood was the railway, was undoubtedly commercially sound; the assets were worth more as sale items than as a going concern! However, with a forebearance to which all lovers of the 'Romney' must be indebted, Mr Lye decided to allow the consortium extra time to raise the money required. Various local meetings were held to arouse support and it was clear that local opinion was very strongly in favour of the railway continuing in its existing form if possible. Local people even formed the Hythe Light Railway Trust to purchase shares in the undertaking if required.

The negotiations dragged on through the autumn of 1971 but meanwhile a fairly notable and purely railway event was taking place. Forty-six years previously *Green Goddess* had run her trials on the Ravenglass & Eskdale Railway; now the directors of that line were considering building a new locomotive and they wanted to know if a six-coupled design would do what they wanted. Mr Lye, still then in control of the railway, agreed that a Romney engine could once again journey to Ravenglass for trials and the choice fell on *Northern Chief*. This may have been fortuitous. The railway would have liked to send *Southern Maid*, then almost fresh out of shops, but the length of her big tender precluded it; only the *Chief* still retained her original short Greenly tender which might just fit on the small R & ER turntables. Nonetheless it was fitting that the other of the original two locomotives should emulate her more famous sister and *Northern Chief* travelled up (by road, alas) in a blaze of placards and publicity; Driver Whawell went with her to ensure that all would go well.

Once settled down and with one or two minor snags ironed out, *Northern Chief* was able to give a very good account of herself. Quite clearly the big-wheeled Pacific was by no means ideal for the Eskdale road but she performed well enough to justify the six-coupled idea in the eyes of the railway management and her superior ride was a revelation. The writer knows and admires the R & ER locos well but from personal experience, the *Chief* on her laminated springs rode like a bogie coach in comparison. By design or accident, she was at Ravenglass over a weekend when that railway played host to the staffs of many other narrow gauge lines, so her visit aroused even more interest than it might otherwise have done. Highlight, perhaps, was the double-headed special on Sunday 8 November when two of Henry Greenly's most magnificent creations, *River Esk* and *Northern Chief,* took a train up and down the valley. It was not strictly necessary —either locomotive could have handled the light train on its own despite appalling weather—but it was a unique occasion.

Meanwhile, back at New Romney, negotiations were proceeding in fits and starts. Even while these were in progress, the existing owners decided that the railway would run again in 1972 whatever happened, so that the staff felt less insecure, and on 14 February 1972, the enthusiast group—loosely known as 'The Consortium'— finally acquired the railway. Since the railway company is a company incorporated under Act of Parliament, and has various restrictions on its financial arrangements, the new owners formed the RH & D Light Railway Holding Company Ltd. This is in existence for the sole purpose of holding the existing shares of the railway company and for providing financial support. It has acquired some 50,450 of the original 51,000 shares, having a total of some 32 shareholders at the time of writing, and is empowered to appoint the directorate of the operating company.

THE PRESENT DAY

As recorded above, the new owners took over on 14 February 1972, Mr J. B. Snell being appointed as managing director, while P. C. Hawkins and G. A. Barlow were confirmed in their existing posts. No doubt enthusiasts expected very great changes to happen almost at once but the new owners very sensibly decided to take stock of the situation before committing themselves to further expenditure on major projects. The year 1972 was in essence a holding year, devoted mainly to trying to remedy some of the many effects of deferred maintenance that were becoming glaringly obvious. The worst of the existing buildings at Dungeness and New Romney received urgent repairs and a coat of paint; an urgent programme of coaching stock repairs was undertaken while studies were initiated in the design of a new standard coach; *Samson*, in pieces again for over a year, was overhauled and reassembled, while Cushing Engineering Ltd of Rainham, Kent were entrusted with, first, the overhaul of the mechanical parts of *Doctor Syn* and then with a complete rebuild of *Hurricane*. More Sierra Leone rail was acquired, the small track-relaying programme started by Mr Lye was extended and extensive experiments are being made with both Jarrahwood and steel sleepers.

With a season's operating experience behind it, the consortium was able, by spring 1973, to sort out priorities. Noteworthy are: the decision to concentrate on large scale production of a handsome new standard coach, while keeping in repair the best of the existing stock; the experiments being made with oil firing in the hope of increasing cleanliness and cutting down shed work; and the adoption of a steady programme of track-relaying. Fairly high priority is also being given to insertion of a passing loop at Maddieson's Camp and to the rebuilding of Hythe and New Romney stations both to provide more imposing entrances to the railway and to give covered storage space for coaches during the winter. A non-contributory staff pension scheme was instituted in 1973.

Inevitably with enthusiasts in charge being watched by other enthusiasts almost any decision to alter the status quo comes under close critical examination. Notable among changes so far, if comment is any guide, have been the reversion to a brown and cream stock livery and the adoption of distinctly non-Greenly building colours of yellow ochre and brown. No doubt the wholesale rebuilding of stations and various other projects that may affect hallowed items will also arouse controversy. Whether such criticisms are valid or just carping, only time will tell. The new owners are obviously taking seriously their responsibilities in making the railway as efficient and as nearly commercially viable as possible. If one reflects at this time that they have much in common with the attitude of Howey and

Greenly, in that they obviously delight in having a whole railway to play with, this is not a criticism. If that attitude had not been present in 1925 there would have been no RH & D; if it had not survived in 1971, neither would the Romney. The new regime cannot really be assessed for a decade or more.

CHAPTER 7

A Trip Round The Line

AROUND NEW ROMNEY

The Romney Hythe & Dymchurch Railway, as its name suggests, was always planned to start from New Romney, and New Romney station is still very much the heart of the line. It seems, therefore, sensible to take the route in two parts starting from there: New Romney to Hythe, and New Romney to Dungeness. When one thinks of the line it is important not to let oneself be deceived by the small size and scale appearance of its stock. This is no miniature seaside railway; its operating problems are those of a full size concern and the engineman (for there is no fireman) is fully occupied with the constant changes of gradient, the many road crossings and the operating problems of an intensive service. Remember too that he is often responsible for the safety of over 200 people and that speeds relative to train weight and braking power are fairly high.

New Romney itself is a full size station in all but gauge. Its exterior frontage to Littlestone Road is modest but inside is a four-platform terminus-cum-through station, its running lines properly protected by interlocked points and signals and its precincts properly equipped with extensive carriage sidings, locomotive sheds, and repair shops, and all the plant needed to maintain a railway. In season it will put five or six locomotives in steam daily, more than most other tourist railways in these islands, and its store of coaching stock is sufficient to make up five 200-passenger rakes.

Yet New Romney, although the hub of the system, is really only an introduction to its hinterland through which the railway runs— the wide expanses of Romney Marsh and the odd shingle banks of the Dungeness peninsular. The whole area has, alas, been somewhat marred by indiscriminate development but is still one of the most

84

emotive parts of England if only for the history and eeriness of the vast Romney Marsh that still stretches away inland. The marsh has many moods and is different in each. The Dungeness road seems to require a blustery, cloud-swept day to recapture at all the original wild aspect of its now despoiled peninsular. On the other hand, for me the ideal time for a run to Hythe is one of those not-too-rare fine evenings in summer when the sunlight lies golden across the corn and the steam drifts gently away, shadowing the pastures with its changing shapes.

A TRIP TO HYTHE

So . . . for Hythe let us join the penultimate working of the day, a short working for which the engine has been gently simmering out beyond the up carriage shed points while an earlier arrival occupies the station roads with its shunting. With the road clear, the Pacific—invariably immaculate whatever its livery—collects its train from the siding and propels it slowly into platform four. Indeed, whatever the time of day your train to Hythe may well start from platform three or four, the 'Dungeness Roads', because only one of the terminal roads is conveniently situated for access to the up line. It may in fact have run in from Dungeness with just a few minutes pause either to change the locomotive or to take on water; but it is more likely to be short working now that the former shuttles—conditional extras—have been incorporated into the main timetable.

To the initiated the start gives an indication of what is to come. All the RH & D intermediate stations seem coincidentally to be in hollows; New Romney is, of course, so because of the need to tunnel beneath Littlestone Road on the Dungeness extension. Hence the line starts with a surprisingly stiff little bank up past the signal box and locomotive sheds. The exact gradient varies but on a rainy day it is quite enough to make starting a heavy train something of a ticklish operation. On a fine sunny evening, however, the locomotive has no trouble in breasting the short bank and as we head out onto the marsh its slow well-spaced beats gradually blur into the characteristic rapid-fire bark of a Greenly Pacific at speed, so different from the measured blasts of, say, the Eskdale locomotives.

To the left, past Greenly's Bungalow set back among trees, is a wide space of railway land, reminder of the original route which curved round hard against the boundary fence; here, after Henry Greenly left, Colonel Tyrrel, another miniature railway enthusiast, had a 7½in gauge line on the old right-of-way, terminating in a turntable where it rejoins the present track. The latter heads out across the agriculural land of the marsh over 'Carey's Sewer,' one of the frequent drainage ditches in these parts, and then starts a gentle climb through the Warren. At this point Henry Greenly had to pass under the main Hythe-New Romney road which he did with a neat two-arched concrete structure still standing although widened in 1973. The railway describes a long lazy-S curve to keep the bridge as short as possible and then climbs on to a summit in a shallow cutting. Emerging, it enters the second part of the 'S', a long right-hand curve dropping gently to Blackhut Bridge; like so many Romney names it is a reminder of times gone by when the little sewer now culverted was open, and a big blackened wood hut stood in one of those odd little triangles of railway land acquired when the route cut across the corner of a field. This still one of the least spoiled sections of the route, with farmland to left and right, and the line begins to climb, again in a sweeping left hander, to gain the famous bridge over the New Sewer. It used to travel straight on, at the expense of a much sharper reverse curve just before the bridge, but was relocated early in 1929—some say in a fit of post-Greenly pique. In winter, or when the land is down to pasture, the old curve can be clearly seen in a field to the left.

The reasons for all the curves are uncertain. There is a long-established story that Greenly liked seeing trains on curves and was busily designing curves into his route wherever possible. He had got as far as 'Duke of York's' when Captain Howey, so it is said, called a summary halt to the proceedings. It's a nice story but there are, on the ground, good civil engineering reasons for all the curviness up to here. They enable the main road at Warren to be crossed almost on the square and in the same way the long sweeping reverse curves up to New Sewer give a bridge only slightly on the skew and only 60-odd feet long. A straight run into St Mary's Bay would have meant a bridge very much on the skew and nearer 90ft long.

When first built, the Duke of York's Bridge was an impressive lattice girder structure; since 1968 its replacement, named after S. H. Collins who ordered it, is far less visually impressive since its girders are below rail level but is still the biggest engineering work on the railway. It marks the top of yet another little bank and once over the top our train's rhythm quickens as it drops down through the right handed Piggery Curve—another Romney ghost since the pig farm is long gone and only the derelict foundations remain in scrubby land to the left. To the right across a field is the former Duke of York's holiday camp and then we are slowing past a clutter of buildings to cross a minor road on the level and enter St Mary's Bay station—alias Jesson, alias Holiday Camp.

St Mary's Bay, so called since 1946, is simply two concrete 'platforms' and a couple of buildings on the up-side. The booking office is an obvious Greenly original but there is something slightly odder about the long high shelter that covers most of the plaform's length. The answer is that it was built about 1950 from pieces of the former carriage shed over New Romney arrival platforms and that in turn was adapted from the original paint shop—Greenly thrice removed as one might say! It is certainly necessary since the surrounding holiday camps generate quite a lot of traffic in the peak season. The minor road, almost unused when the railway was built, is now a busy link and its crossing must be flagged.

As usual the station is in a dip and the enginemen do not exactly welcome the longish bank to Golden Sands, though the slow start gives passengers plenty of time to admire the long line of the Kentish Downs just coming into view on the left across pleasant farmland. Our right is occupied entirely by the huge Golden Sands Holiday Centre with its rows of little stuccoed chalets and its small walled platform on the down-side—really an alcove rather than a station, although it still handles a fair amount of traffic for the weekly shoppers' trips to Hythe and other special workings. Just at the end of the camp the gradient levels out at Golden Sands bridge, where the line crosses Cobsden Sewer. Indeed, the bridge itself used to be two inches higher at the Dymchurch end and a recent renewal on the level has meant quite a sharp inclination at the southern end; looking back along the train one can distinctly see the roof line altering as successive coaches top the grade and the strain on the locomotive eases for the level sprint into Dymchurch. We are coming in parallel to the coast here and only a rash of new bungalows separates the line from the famous Dymchurch Wall that keeps the sea at bay. Fields and a sewage works give advance warning of Dymchurch itself with the inevitable drop down over a flagged crossing into the pretty station.

Dymchurch (Marshlands) as it was once known, has been markedly improved over the last few years. Its overall roof is neatly painted and whitewashed to make the best of the thick concrete blast walls put on by the Army and the lawns and gardens at the Hythe end are trim and well cared for. Even the former bay, now reduced to a short spur, is neatly raked over and the colour light signals—for this is a block section—if not as handsome as the old semaphores, are much more convenient operationally. Yet some features have disappeared from view almost entirely. Only the forewarned will catch a glimpse of the former tearooms, now a bungalow hidden behind the up-side wall, or note the tell-tale concrete ring behind a fence on the down-side marking the old turntable well. Dymchurch village is mainly out to the seaward side.

Dymchurch, of course, is in a dip. The train starts more or less on the level, across a wide sewer and a dangerous flagged crossing but just as the engineman has got it rolling nicely it hits a marked bank.

These little banks, of 1 in 1,000 down to about 1 in 125 may seem chickenfeed to a main line driver, but with trains of up to 60 tons—over five times the engine's own weight—they represent a considerable challenge to the somewhat light-footed Pacifics and one which calls for considerable skill on the part of the enginemen. This one lasts over Fehr's crossing, an occupation track named after its owner, and right up to Hoorne's Sewer bridge, where it eases. It is a definite slog in this direction, although something of a relief to hard-pressed down trains which know they are over the worst for a while once they have breasted Hoorne's. The stretch is not one of the most interesting on the line, with only scrubby fields, trees and some very mixed development on its seaward side, although the downs stretching straight along the western horizon are beginning to make their presence felt.

Once over Hoorne's Sewer we drop again to pass the broken strips of concrete that now mark the site of defunct Burmarsh Road, whistling insistently and slowing for the unguarded road crossing at its northern end. Just past here the railway route cuts right through a former small-holding and the two parts provide interesting contrasts. On the left is decaying grass and shrubs, but on the right a batch of brand new bungalows—the owner one imagines has probably not lost very much!

With the last houses left behind the line climbs inevitably but gently over open marshlands, with only a long concrete access road accompanying it to the left and a clear view across seaward to Dymchurch Wall. The 'summit', if so one can call it, was formerly marked by an obvious and complicated feature where four dykes or sewers joined, known as Star Dyke. Confusingly, it is still referred to

Page 89 (above) Green Goddess *with a trial train on the Ravenglass & Eskdale Railway on 3 July 1925;* (below) Northern Chief *passes through Irton Road, R & ER, November 1971*

Page 90 *New Romney station from the air, 1972. The site of the former SR siding runs alongside the road and ends in the foundations of 'Dunrobin's Shed'. The locomotive*

as such though two dykes are now piped, the other two dry so that only a few depressions by the first curve out of Burmarsh give the site away! Now the engine can be eased again past the gate and field-path that act as a halt for the Beach Holiday Camp, with a long and very gentle downgrade to where the marsh's main sewage plant stands solitary beside the Willop Sewer.

THE GALLOPING GROUND

The clickety-click of wheels on staggered joints always seems to accelerate as we clatter across the Willop for, even if subconsciously, the drivers know this as the galloping ground on which most of the railway's speed attempts have been carried out. From the summit near Star Dyke there is a steady drop to provide acceleration and from the Willop the line falls very gently towards Hythe in a straight line for almost a mile. On this stretch Captain Howey achieved the figure of 60.2mph in the Rolls Royce and, so he once confessed, almost frightened himself to death when he worked *Hurricane* up to nearly 35mph before having to brake extremely sharply for Botolph's Bridge Road. Even service trains have been known to break out of the Pacific's comfortable 22–3mph lope, and speed to rise into the middle twenties, but higher speeds are not encouraged. Nowadays the trains must slow sharply before New Cut which is followed closely by the unguarded crossing of Botolph's Bridge Road. The former halt site is recognisable only from a slight widening of the formation, though doubtless the foundations of its former shelter lie among the scrub on the up-side. Again, the line drops sharply past Botolph's Bridge and often on this stretch one has the excitement of passing another train on the double track. Anyone who still thinks of the RH & D as only a toy has only to look ahead on such an occasion to realise it is no such thing and the combined closing speed of the two trains is well over 40mph.

As we cross the Palmarsh flats, the downland ridge known as Lympne Hills cuts in from the left, becoming very prominent and looming well above us (Lympne Castle is almost out of sight now, buried among its woods). On the right are first the working part of West Hythe ballast pits and then the flooded Palmarsh pits that supplied much of the railway's original ballast. A group of shrubs and a kink in the fence to seaward mark the site of Palmarsh signal box as we swing first right and then left in a huge lazy-S curve to drop

F

beneath the road at Prince of Wales Bridge. Greenly's original handsome two-arched structure—more a tunnel than a bridge—raises the road some feet above the former level but the railway is nevertheless very much in a dip. With a heavy train the gradient out of the bridge in either direction can be a testing moment for the enginemen.

ENTRY TO HYTHE

We are now well within the outer suburbs of Hythe as the downs, blocking the western skyline, and the military canal swing in parallel to the railway on the left; no doubt it would be more accurate to describe the railway as swinging in parallel, but that is not the impression one gets from a fast moving train! The downs and canal stay with us all through the run in to Hythe, past the 'S-bend' and beside new houses and old factories to reach the line's terminus. There is little of note besides the municipal refuse destructor! But Hythe station itself somehow retains a pretty setting. Much as Greenly designed it, save for lengthened roof and odd track amendments, it makes quite an imposing finish to the journey—provided one comes by train. The road aspect is much less imposing although it has recently been much improved by rebuilding.

NEW ROMNEY—DUNGENESS

The Dungeness extension was an afterthought and that much is obvious in the way it commences. The need to dive under Littlestone Road puts the line in a dip at New Romney, and trains are faced with a continuous climb for almost half-a-mile from a standing start. Indeed, the brick- and concrete-lined cutting looks most impressive from above and smoke eddies in main-line fashion from the twin tunnels as the train moves slowly off.

Once out of the tunnel we ease onto the single line, passing almost immediately the remains of the short-lived 'Littlestone up' station, its crumbling building set back into a bank by the platform area. The prominent bridge abutments are not those of the former footbridge but once supported a sheepbridge connecting a lane to the old SR station to our right. The former SR trackbed parallels us on the up-side behind a screen of trees while industrial clutter and a ballast crushing plant block the seaward view. There used to be a spur into the works. Its derelict embankment, dropping in to a trailing junction, can still be discerned as the engine whistles for the grandiloquently named Church Lane crossing, a green track that marks the beginning of Half-Mile Curve. This is a sweeping left-hander that eventually brings the line out on a low embankment and over a summit before another track, prosaically named Half-Mile Crossing.

Thence we drop gently through newish developments to the extensive patch of ground which is all that remains of Greatstone Dunes Station. All too clearly, Greenly anticipated far more development here than has taken place even now—it was after all going to be a 'Garden City in the Sands' or so the brochures said. Now it is a decaying halt with a nameboard, all that is left of the original plan being parts of a Greenly shelter walled up in an army pillbox; the latter is so stout it has survived not only the vandals who smashed the rest, but also the demolition efforts of railway staff.

As usual, Greatstone is in a dip—and apparently deliberately so since Greenly's gradient diagrams show 1 in 1,000 up in either direction. Something has happened to the shingle, since there is now a climb at nearer 1 in 400 up to the nearby road crossing and out into scenery typical of the coastal strip today—scattered new developments on the weedy shingle, and a single row of houses facing the coast road and seawall; the developments get more shacklike as one nears Dungeness itself.

This road crossing illustrates one problem for the railway—the way in which new housing is constantly threatening to erode the already barely adequate sightliness for approaching trains. The railway would ideally like 90ft clear along the road as well as 90ft along the railway, but has had to settle for 60–90ft—and even that is being cut down in places. Beyond the crossing, however, the housing is set well back at each side and the line runs over clear shingle almost up to the neat cream and blue enclosures that are Littlestone Holiday Camp (now known after its owners as 'Maddieson's'). Maddieson's halt, an enclosed strip by the camp's main entrance, is a booked stop and available for public use; it is also, now, a crossing place with a long loop. Dungeness trains carry a travelling guard so anyone intending to alight will already have been seen by the train crew and the engineman warned.

The start from Maddieson's is on a gentle rise of about 1 in 1,000 but it is not steep enough to notice: trains just run more freely in the Hythe direction. The line starts over largely cleared land with open views to the west across the shingle, of which the peninsular is largely composed. Over the derelict SR trackbed, some way inland, can be seen the grey outlandish shapes of old concrete 'mirrors'— relics of the pre-war War Department experiments with parabolic sound-reflectors that provided the RH & D with one of its many branches. There are several dish-like structures scattered over the marsh and the nearby downs but the most impressive is the big rectangular curtain-wall affair that stands parallel to the railway some distance away. Directly in line with this is a small bridge under the former SR branch and the road leading through that bridge was originally the trackbed of the 'WD branch' whose junction, facing to Romney, can still be seen climbing steeply to meet the present line. The ballast pits it served later are out of sight behind the SR, but their flooded workings effectively cut off access to the old WD property.

Immediately after this, the line once more plunges between newish residential development on both sides, passing under one of two bridges erected about 1937–8 to emerge on the shingle again. We are now very close to the sea, the shingle beach with its boats being clearly visible just beyond a row of houses and bungalows and the untidy mess continues right up to Lade. Lade is two awkward road crossings, passed with much slowing and whistling, and a small concrete shelter by the Lade Stores. Foundations of the inevitable Greenly building can be seen half obscured by the new one.

From Lade on, the developments get scrappier and more untidy, their rawness pointed up by the good architectural manners of a group of old coastguard cottages to landward. Many of the older tarred shacks belong to the fishermen whose boats can be seen drawn up at intervals along the shingle, with little tramlines beside them running down to the sea. Formerly the tracks extended in some cases to the RH & D; now they stop at the coast road.

What remains of the bleak scenery is now gone for ever, dwarfed by the towering bulk of Dungeness Atomic Power Station. Dungeness A already overshadows the old lighthouse installations, Dungeness B is rising alongside, while harsh lines of pylons slash across the marsh skyline. The railway itself was moved bodily inland on this stretch at some time before the war, presumably to help the housing developers on its seaward side, and it runs parallel to its old route down to Kerton Road Bridge. Kerton Road is the second of the extension bridges, a very basic steel and concrete structure erected about 1937, and the railway dips beneath it then climbs gently to

The Pilot. As already mentioned, this was the terminus for several months and soon after Kerton Road the trackbed of a former turning triangle is still clearly laid out on the shingle for the 'initiates' to see. The Pilot Inn, which gives the halt its name is some 300 yards further on, by a level crossing, a concrete shelter and the inevitable Greenly foundations. Thence the line drops over the minor road down towards its terminus, diverging from the coast as it does so. The huge balloon loop that contains Dungeness terminus can be clearly seen from a low embankment that leads to the spring loaded loop points known as Britannia Points.

If you wonder why they are called that, the explanation is typically 'Romney'. The original Britannia Inn used to be here until it was burned down just after the war; the present one, established in a huddle of ex-army buildings right by the lighthouse, is simply its successor.

The train slows to run straight ahead through the loop points and run clockwise round Dungeness loop, alternately on embankment and in cutting. The skyline ahead is an untidy jumble of new and old lighthouses, shacks, old railway coaches and the power station installation. In front of them across the arc of loop can be seen the modest station buildings of the RH & D and the derelict shells of former weigh-houses; the embankment of a short-lived branch to them is just discernable on the left as the train emerges from a shallow cutting and brakes for the station. End of journey: the RH & D station, now a long shelter backed by a café and a small booking office, is right in the shadow of the former lighthouse and hard by the remains of the old SR station.

Foundations of Greenly buildings, sleeper marks of old standard gauge sidings and the odd van body litter the area to tantalise the industrial archaeologist, but basically the railway ends here. There remains only the long sweeping curve through shingle that will bring the train once more to Britannia Points and head it again towards Hythe. The sea is only a hundred yards away and one can sit on the steep bank and watch the ships which come close inshore here until it is time to return—or unless it is a really fine day, refresh oneself more comfortably at the Britannia or the railway café.

CHAPTER 8

Steam Locomotives and Petrol Tractors

STEAM LOCOMOTIVES

The Romney Hythe & Dymchurch Railway is unusual among British minor railways in that, with one short-lived exception, its stud of steam locomotives has always been of one basic design, and is the design work of one man—Henry Greenly. The nine locomotives comprise seven Pacific (4–6–2) tender machines and two Mountains (4–8–2). All were bought new during the early years, and all are still in service.

The basic design
The basic Pacific design—that which later materialised as RH & D Nos 1, 2 and 3—can reasonably be taken as the culmination of all Greenly's locomotive work. By the time he was asked, in 1924, to design a large express locomotive for Count Zborowski and Captain Howey, he had some twenty years' experience behind him; the Bassett-Lowke Little Giants and *Gigantic* had shown the problems of providing power to normal scale in 15in gauge; the performance of those locomotives and a slightly modified *Gigantic* on the Ravenglass & Eskdale Railway had shown the structural problems of true scale models in hard service; and the design of the massive 2–8–2 *River Esk*, also for the R & ER, had, while providing its own headaches, given convincing proof of the advantages to be gained from building 'over-scale' and to a freelance design. Thus, when Zborowski and Howey commissioned him to design a strong fast express locomotive Greenly had a very good basis on which to work—in retrospect the only regret is that *Esk* had not been in service long enough to show up certain design defects (eg, the coil springing) that became incorporated in the new design. It must be remembered here that

the original two locomotives were built without any definite destination in mind, although it appears a long line was visualised; the comments below, however, to save confusion, will refer to all locomotives as RH & D machines, since the description details refer to all of these in general.

To return to the basic 'RH & D' design, both Greenly and Captain Howey were admirers of the work of Mr (later Sir) Nigel Gresley, then CME of the London and North Eastern Railway. In particular they were very impressed by Gresley's new 'Great Northern'* type Pacific locomotives and it was therefore natural that a similar outline and general design should be adopted for the new 15in gauge machine. They resembled closely their 'prototypes', and adopted several Gresley features—for example the 'Cartazzi' system of radial axle boxes for the trailing carrying axles to avoid the complication of a separate truck. At the same time the adoption of a 'scale' of 1:3 instead of the more accurate (for the gauge) 1:4, together with associated practical design considerations, made the locomotives different enough to have a distinctive 'Greenly' stamp about them; the visible change is mainly to do with the proportions which are subtly different, giving a slightly greater height-to-length ratio that somehow looks 'right' in this size—it is sufficiently different that when, as a recent experiment, a plan was drawn up for 'streamlining' one, the 'A4' type casing proposed did not give the classic A4 outline. It looked too high and short.

As designed, therefore, the two original locomotives built simultaneously were handsome 4–6–2s of generally GN outline with neat bogie tenders and parallel boilers; they were, according to the working drawings, intended to have tapered boiler lagging but this feature was omitted by the manufacturers Davey Paxman Ltd. The firebox was of the widegrate Wootton variety extending right across the frames and a rather peculiar gridiron steam drier much favoured by Greenly was fitted in the smokebox to provide a moderate degree of superheating. Unlike their three-cylindered prototypes the engines had only two, outside, cylinders with Walschaerts valve gear and were originally fitted with both vacuum and Westinghouse brakes.

It is not exactly clear why Davey Paxman, of Colchester, was chosen to build these machines. Count Zborowski who actually ordered both of them as described in chapter two was apparently a friend of Paxman which may have influenced the placing of the

*Designed for the GNR but mostly built for its successor the LNER.

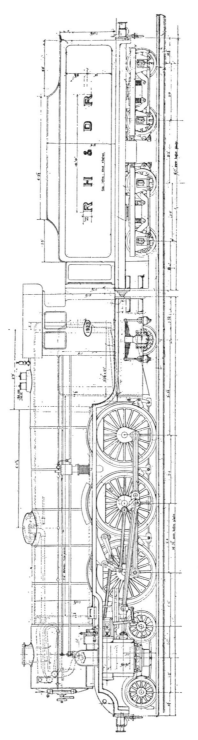

GA drawing of Greenly's original design for the 4-6-2 (GEC Diesels Ltd)

contract; on the other hand, Greenly had already worked with Paxman's in producing the *River Esk*. There is some evidence that the contract was to some extent a keenly priced one—certainly where the evidence was not visible some of Greenly's elegant design curves were 'brutalised' into simpler but cheaper angles, and such details as the taper boiler lagging were not included. On the whole, however, the locomotives were extremely well built and a credit to their makers.

As built the locomotives showed both the strength and weaknesses of their designer. Henry Greenly was first and foremost a model engineer and although he had obviously learnt a lot from previous work he still tended to work 'upwards' from the model idea: the characteristic shows plainly in all his works, for example, even in such large projects as the granite crushing plant at Murthwaite on the R & ER which was a superb piece of model engineering but not really up to hard work—it was too finely engineered! In this he was no doubt hampered by his background: his friend and German contemporary, Roland Martens of Krauss (Munich) was a light railway locomotive designer and his contemporary Pacific designs show the advantages of working 'downwards'. Martens tended to adopt full-size practice in detail work, Greenly if in doubt adopted the current model practice. Hence the 'gridiron' superheater which was a model idea that did not work satisfactorily in this scale, and the provision of coil springs (concealed within dummy laminated ones on the radial axle) rather than the real thing. While they may have been all right on garden railways, they were not suited to the kind of high-speed long-haul work for which the new locomotives were intended. Nor was the weight balance quite right; indeed all Greenly's big locomotive designs were and are rather 'light on their feet', a factor attributable partly to suspension design and partly to general weight distribution: however it is probably not really fair to blame their designer overmuch. Many more eminent locomotive engineers have met the same problem and small changes in the weight distribution in a light 15in gauge machine are considerably more critical than in a full size locomotive. On the other hand Greenly's previous experience also provided the many good features in the locomotives: they were designed with more than adequate strength in all their major components, the boiler was a good steam producer and, once minor details had been sorted out, the front end design with its Cluipet-ringed piston valves was extremely efficient; a Greenly Pacific in good condition uses surprisingly little steam to move an average length train. The general design was clean and made for easy maintenance. Probably the greatest tribute to their designer is that they have lasted so long under such arduous service conditions.

An interesting point in their design, reflecting Greenly's readiness to explore advanced ideas, was that the original two machines were designed so that they could be oil-fired—it is said, at the count's instance. Until the boxes were patched in 1946 there was a tube passing through the rear water space of the firebox beneath the firebox door, so that a burner and fuel lead could be inserted. It was blanked off by plates from the start and was never used but the provision was there. It was a constant source of leakage before being patched.

As related in chapter two the two original locomotives were taken over by Captain Howey after Count Zborowski's death and sold to the RH & D company (a paper transfer) as their first locomotives; a third identical machine was ordered direct from Davey Paxman in 1926 to provide a spare machine and a small 0-4-0T with tender was bought ready-made from Krauss of Munich for construction work: this will be described fully on page 106. As the RH & D project grew, with the prospect of double line right through to Hythe and the hopes of goods traffic, it became clear that more power would be needed. Accordingly Henry Greenly produced a 4-8-2 variant of the basic design with a slightly longer boiler and smaller coupled wheels; it was still Great Northern in appearance although otherwise freelance. Two were ordered from Davey Paxman for goods services and an additional two Pacifics were ordered at the same time. These were different from the originals in one major respect. Captain Howey appears to have wanted some really powerful locomotives and, no doubt inspired by Gresley's locomotives, Greenly designed a three-cylinder version of his own Pacific, the third cylinder being identical in size to the outside ones and operated by Greenly's own design of radial valve gear. Otherwise the engines were identical to the earlier ones and the boiler had no difficulty in supplying the necessary steam. All were delivered in time for the opening, Nos 5–8 were built together as a batch following on directly from No 3 and the works numbers ran consecutively from 16040 to 16044. Vacuum brake was standardised on all locomotives before opening.

In the intensive and high speed service that quickly developed owing to public demand, the various small design defects became apparent. In particular the coil springing particularly on the radial axles caused the locomotives to roll badly at speed and Mr A. A.

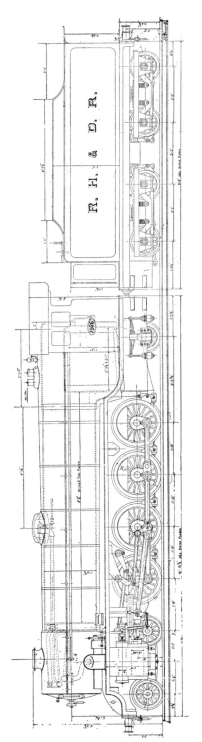

GA drawing of Greenly's original design for the 4-8-2 (GEC Diesels Ltd)

Binfield clearly recalls being stationed on a flat truck in front of No 5 and being told to see if the wheels actually left the rails . . . apparently they did, once or twice, which cannot have been very good for his peace of mind! This actually took place after Greenly had left but once the fault was located it was quickly put right. All the Pacifics had their coil springs on the coupled wheels replaced by working laminated ones over a very short period of time and the ride was drastically improved. The 4–8–2s proved more intractable since their design gave little room for any modification except for the fitting of laminated springs on the trailing axleboxes; since they were not expected to maintain such high speeds and since, with smaller wheels and longer wheelbases, they were in any case steadier, coil springs for the coupled wheels were retained and are there to this day. The various other minor defects were gradually sorted out. Some lingered on, like the steam driers which were one of Greenly's pet ideas; they did not go until he left but did not long survive his departure. As with Gresley's engines, the inside cylinders and motion of Nos 7 and 8 gave considerable maintenance problems but they were persevered with until the mid-1930s.

The opening of the Dungeness extension brought a demand for extra locomotive power. At first it was intended to order two more Pacifics from Davey Paxman and they were even allocated serial numbers (16692–3); interestingly enough, they were to be two-cylindered, so the more complicated design of Nos 7 and 8 was obviously giving trouble even then. Instead there materialised what must be regarded as the final flowering of his 15in gauge design, an improved Pacific that incorporated all the lessons learnt over the previous three years. As related in chapter three it is uncertain just how much say Greenly actually had in the planning of these loco-motives but in practice his chassis design was used almost complete except for the substitution of a rear pony truck for the Cartazzi radial axle. The Roland Martens-designed boiler undoubtedly incorporated much experience gained from Greenly's work and thus in these machines one can see a blending of the best features of the two leading miniature locomotive designers of the period. The handsome Canadian-style outline was probably due mainly to Howey and while Greenly had, earlier in 1928, talked of the advantages of trans-atlantic practice in robustness, ease of maintenance and driver protection, he had specifically mentioned *American*-type locomotives such as he had previously designed for Jackson, Rigby. Nos 9 and 10 were definitely

Canadian, and based on the light Pacifics of the Canadian National Railway. Their usual attribution of Canadian Pacifics originally came from references to Canadian (style) Pacifics and had nothing to do with the railway of that name, but the common references to them as 'CPRs' followed naturally!

In design, then, the locomotives were mechanically similar to the earlier ones as modified but had slightly higher-pitched taper boilers developed by Roland Martens of Krauss from those of his very successful German-style Pacifics of 1925; they had handsome blued-steel lagging and top-mounted sandboxes.

The tenders were of the Vanderbilt type with a high-set coal bunker fronting a long cylindrical water tank and incorporated vacuum-operated water scoops; there was apparently a project for installing water troughs near Greatstone but it never came to fruition. Other 'American' features were bells on the boiler tops, cow-catchers or pilots, and dummy push-pole sockets on the buffer beams, presumably for the sake of verisimilitude. In American full scale practice these were used when pole-shunting vehicles on an adjacent siding but there is no evidence that this was ever seriously contemplated at New Romney.

It was originally intended to build these engines at New Romney but as related in chapter three the existing parts were despatched to the Yorkshire Engine Company. That concern appears to have completed these two locomotives more or less 'by eye' since no drawings were available. Certainly the locomotives differ in minor details and the job, no doubt done as occasion offered, took over two years.

Notes on the histories of individual locomotives are given below; all have had partial or complete rebuilds at various times, all but two have received new tenders. Apart from the early modifications and the 'down grading' of 7 and 8 to two-cylinder machines in 1935 and 1937 respectively, the only major alteration has been the provision of new parallel boilers between 1956 and 1964 to *all* locomotives including Nos 9 and 10. These boilers retain the basic Greenly design and dimensions but are properly superheated with two twin elements each. Modern superheating has certainly improved both the engines' performance and their fuel consumption although it is questionable whether anything available in Greenly's day would have had the same effect. Hindsight always makes it easier to find the weak points in a design! Note that only major overhauls are described below.

Routine maintenance including such items as retubing, wheel tyring etc is of course carried out at regular intervals.

Individual Locomotives

No 1 *Green Goddess*. GN outline 4–6–2
Davey Paxman 15469 of 1925

Green Goddess was the first Pacific to be completed, being delivered to Captain Howey in April or May 1925; she was named after a favourite play of her owner. She ran trials on the Ravenglass & Eskdale Railway during June of that year, achieving 'all that could be desired' (see appendix three) and was then stored at New Romney until work started on the railway. She was originally fitted with both vacuum brake and Westinghouse air-brake equipment, early photographs clearly showing the Westinghouse pump, and was occasionally used on railway construction. The Westinghouse brake was removed when the vacuum brake was standardised before July 1927 and the locomotive played its full part in running the railway up to the war. In 1946 it was overdue for shopping and was rebuilt at Ashford Works, Southern Railway during winter 1946–7; in particular the firebox was repaired, the boiler retubed and a new high capacity bogie tender provided. Since then the major item of note has been a new superheated boiler by Gowers of Bedford, fitted in 1956. The last major overhaul was in 1960. It may be worth noting that in many ways *Green Goddess* has since the war replaced *Hurricane* as the premier engine of the line—ie the one the public associate with it. This is probably due to the fact that for over 26 years she has been the 'personal' engine of the railway's operating manager and longest employed driver, George Barlow. *Green Goddess* has always borne a green livery: her initial livery was the 'standard' one of lined LNER green but the colour has varied over the years. Since 1967 she has been in very pleasant Great Northern apple green shade with white and black lining.

No 2 *Northern Chief*. GN outline two-cylinder Pacific
Davey Paxman 15470 of 1925

This locomotive was originally ordered at the same time as *Green Goddess* and stored with her at New Romney until construction commenced. She was used in line construction and, appropriately, hauled the first official train, on the occasion of the Duke of York's visit on 5 August 1926. As with No 1 she was originally Westinghouse-fitted and her early history is very similar. No 2 has, however, had several minor oddities in her career. In about 1936, she was provided with tapered boiler lagging to a design by Mr Fenn of Walker Fenn 'controlled clockwork' fame; the lagging, which still exists, was to a rather sharper taper than Greenly's original design. She apparently did some work during the war but was in bad condition by 1946; indeed, to keep her going, she was temporarily fitted with No 3's boiler during part of the 1946 season, after that locomotive had sustained damage through an accident at Dymchurch. No 2 received her own retubed boiler later in 1946 and was then rebuilt during the winter of 1947–8 at New Romney. Unlike all the other locomotives except No 6, she retained her original small Greenly tender which was still in use in 1973, albeit rebogied. The original boiler was adapted to take a superheater in 1952 and it was this experiment that led to general reboilering of the locomotive stock. No 2 received a completely new superheated boiler in 1957 and since then has had two shoppings.

In November 1971, *Northern Chief* followed No 1's example and was sent to Ravenglass to run trials on the R & ER; the intention was to assess the merits and demerits of a six-coupled design for that railway. The trials were generally successful and are described in appendix three.

Livery of No 2 has varied over the years. She was originally LNER green, lined out, but was painted black during the war. In October 1946, she was repainted a dark green—officially 'Highland Railway green'—and ran for some seasons like that. She is now Napier green, a rather similar shade.

No 3 *Southern Maid*. GN outline two-cylinder Pacific
Davey Paxman 16040/26 (All the DP locomotives but 1 and 2 carry 1926 plates although they were completed in 1927.)

No 3 was ordered early in 1926 when the need for a third locomotive was first realised, and was delivered on 20 April 1927. Originally she was to be named *Southern Chief*, and official photographs taken at Davey Paxman's show her with this name. For some reason Howey changed his mind and the plates were removed before she entered service. She ran nameless until *Maid* plates were fitted late in 1927 and, as a matter of record, has run nameless on two occasions since; the most confusing was in 1946–7 winter when her plates were 'borrowed' to rename *Hurricane* for an exhibition (qv).

Early history was similar to that of Nos 1 and 2. She was rebuilt at New Romney after the war and fitted with a handsome high-capacity tender supplied by Ashford Works in 1947. She received a superheated boiler in 1957 and was extensively rebuilt at New Romney in 1970–1 when her boiler was fitted with new lagging sheets as closely as possible to Greenly's original tapered design. Like other locomotives on the line she has featured in occasional accidents, her most notable one being a dive into a dyke in 1946, after being rammed by a motor lorry on a level crossing at Dymchurch. No 3 has had the most livery changes of any Romney locomotive. She was originally LNER green but was repainted during the war by the Army in 'Wickham blue', a mid-blue vaguely reminiscent of the Caledonian. In 1946 she once again became green, remaining so until 1954 when she was changed to Brighton umber. In 1959 this was succeeded by a French grey scheme that lasted until 1965 when it was replaced by Malachite green. In 1971 she was painted in GN green with a dark green border and with brown frames. She was fully lined out in black and white which is the current livery.

No 4 *The Bug*. Industrial pattern 0–4–0 tender-tank. Two-cylinder Krauss, Munich, No 6378 of 1926

This locomotive was the odd man out in Romney stock. Ordered in 1926 via Jackson, Rigby Ltd for use in construction and shunting work, she was a standard Krauss design as supplied to a number of miniature railways on the continent. She was a side and well tank locomotive with a separate coal and water tender. The locomotive was fitted with Stephenson's link motion and had only hand brakes. *The Bug* name was carried on cast nameplates. She was delivered in May 1926 and was used in the construction of both the original line and the Dungeness extension. She may have been intended subsequently as a yard shunter at New Romney but work did not justify this and in the early 1930s she was sold to a showman at Blackpool. By March 1934 she had arrived in Belfast to run at a park there and remained there until sold for scrap about 1950. Oddly enough she was not scrapped but simply buried under a pile of junk, her 'grave' becoming something of a pilgrimage spot for miniature railway enthusiasts. She was exhumed in 1969 but considered as irreclaimable and was believed to have been cut up. In actuality it appears only the tender was destroyed, the remains of the locomotive surviving in private hands until bought by Mr W. H. McAlpine in

Page 107 (above) *The exterior of New Romney as originally built;* (left) *A typical Greenly signal box, at New Romney;* (below) *Greenly shelter and nameboard, New Romney*

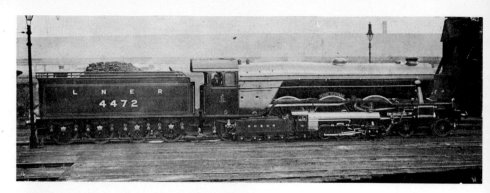

Page 108 (above) *The Giant and the Dwarf; a famous publicity picture, this shows the contrast between a Greenly Pacific and its big brother;* (left) *4–6–2 No 8, Hurricane, as a three-cylinder locomotive. Detail of inside cylinder;* (below) Hurricane *at Hythe, in 1936*

1972 and returned to New Romney. The eventual intention is to rebuild her but it will be a major undertaking. Nevertheless, a new boiler is currently being built.

No 5 *Hercules*. Freelance outline two-cylinder 4–8–2
Davey Paxman 16041/27

No 5 was ordered late in 1926 as one of two goods locomotives. She was built with straight nameplates which Captain Howey disliked; they were replaced with curved ones even though there were no splashers for them to curve round but meanwhile the locomotive ran nameless for some time. In this form she hauled the official opening train. The 4–8–2s were much harder on the curves than the Pacifics so, when the expected goods traffic did not materialise, they were used as little as possible. After the arrival of Nos 9 and 10 they were both withdrawn from service.

Hercules lay derelict, though largely intact, from about 1931 to 1936, when she was rebuilt for use on ballast workings and restored to service in 1936–7. She was used during the war as motive power for the armoured train (see page 63) and was partially clad in mild-steel plate for this duty. In 1946 she was rebuilt at the Southern Railway's Ashford works, receiving a new Ashford-built high capacity tender a little later. This rebuild resulted in a much disfigured appearance since the tender dimensions were misjudged and it towered over the locomotive. The cab roof was raised to try to balance the appearance and the tender flare reduced but the locomotive remained ugly until the tender was rebuilt in 1959. She was fitted with a new superheated boiler in 1958, this boiler being standard with the Pacific ones but with the smokebox extended by seven inches.

Both the 4–8–2s were regularly used after the war since most of the small-radius points had been replaced. *Hercules* in particular was on ballast traffic until about 1948, being temporarily fitted with an electric headlight and generator set for night work, and has since then been used on normal passenger workings. She is reasonably popular although she tends to roll at speed.

Livery was originally LNER green, changed to Malachite in 1946, but from 1954 on she has been painted successively brown and two different shades of red. From 1954–9 she was in Brighton umber, lined yellow; from then until 1968–9 she was in a darkish red officially described as Midland lake, and since then she has been a bright red known as Dahlia red.

G

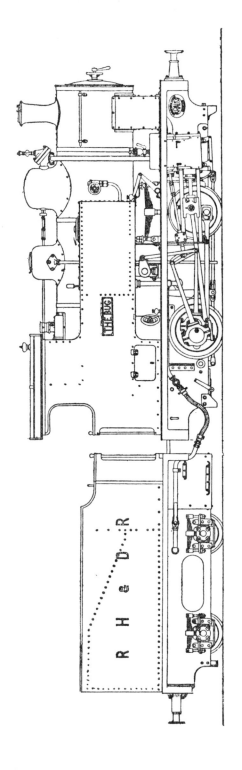

240 TENDER SHUNTING LOCOMOTIVE, No. 4, "THE BUG," ROMNEY, HYTHE & DYMCHURCH RAILWAY, USED FOR CONSTRUCTION OF THE LINE.

The Bug. (RH & DR)

No 6 *Samson*. Freelance outline 4–8–2 two-cylinder
Davey Paxman 16042/27

Samson's early history is similar to that of *Hercules*, although she never ran without nameplates. Like *Hercules* she was withdrawn about 1931, and was used as a spare-parts mine throughout the 1930s. By 1939 she was reduced virtually to a boiler shell and frames without wheels and remained in this state throughout the war. In 1946–7, however, she was completely rebuilt by Clifford Edwards at Hove with various new parts and put back into service in anticipation of ballast traffic. Since her original tender was little used, it was retained and is still (1973) in service. She received a new standard super-heated boiler with extended smokebox in 1961 and was extensively overhauled at New Romney in 1970–2.

Livery was varied. Originally LNER green which deteriorated to plain rust, she was painted Malachite green in 1947. This lasted until 1955 when she was painted lined black, officially Caledonian Railway mixed traffic livery. Since her last overhaul she has been again repainted in the same livery.

In the late 1930s, *Samson* exchanged wheels with *Hercules* and this position has never been rectified.

No 7 *Typhoon*. GN outline Pacific two-cylinder (formerly three-cylinder)
Davey Paxman 16043/27

In accordance with Captain Howey's wish for really powerful locomotives, *Typhoon* was one of two three-cylinder Pacifics built during 1926–7; she was delivered on 19 May 1927 and her early history is similar to that of the other engines. The inside cylinder and motion presented considerable maintenance problems and in 1935–6 she was sent to Davey Paxman for rebuilding as a two-cylinder machine; the third cylinder and steam chest were disconnected and blanked off but left in situ. She was rewheeled at the same time, and tapered boiler lagging was fitted. *Typhoon* then continued normally until the war, during which she was used from time to time by the military. In 1946 she was rebuilt at Ashford Works, retaining her small tender until later that year when a new Ashford-built high capacity one was provided. She was the last of the original Pacifics to receive a superheated boiler, in 1958, and since then has had no major repairs, although by the time this book appears in print she is likely to have received a complete overhaul. Her most distinctive feature was caused by the fitting of a pair of standard industrial Gresham and Craven ejectors in 1965. They are installed just forward of the cab on the left side, being covered by a neat streamlined casing.

Livery was originally LNER green but has been Malachite green from 1946 on.

No 8 *Hurricane*. GN outline Pacific two-cylinder (formerly three-cylinder)
Davey Paxman 16044/27

Delivered on 20 July 1927, *Hurricane* was identical to *Typhoon*. She became the favourite locomotive of Captain Howey who adopted her as his 'own' and drove her frequently in service. Consequently she received preferential treatment such as stainless-steel handrails, acquiring a high capacity tender in 1934 and remaining three-cylinder until the inside motion actually failed in service in July 1937. She was towed back to New Romney and there converted to two-cylinder over the following week, a set of wheels being temporarily borrowed from *Southern Maid*; as with *Typhoon* the third cylinder was disconnected, blanked off and left in situ. Following this incident, Captain Howey became less attached to the locomotive and in 1938 she was painted blue and renamed *Bluebottle*. In this guise she was used on the new Blue Train until the war during which she was used fairly extensively by the Army. In 1946-7 she was put on exhibition at Waterloo Station, SR, carrying *Southern Maid*'s nameplates for the occasion and was rebuilt at Ashford Works during 1947-8, by that time being renamed *Hurricane*. During this rebuild the Cartazzi radial axleboxes and horns were put in the wrong way round, an error which somewhat surprisingly remained undetected until the locomotive 'inexplicably' derailed when entering Hythe. She was reboilered at New Romney in 1956 and overhauled in 1958, remaining in general service until 1971. She was rebuilt during the seasons 1972-3 her third cylinder being at last removed.

Livery was originally LNER green, but was changed to Caledonian blue in 1938. In 1946 she was Wickham blue but for the 1947 season only was repainted light green. After overhaul she became a dark blue similar to Drummond's original Caledonian livery, and in 1958 she was again painted medium (Caledonian) blue.

No 9 *Winston Churchill* (formerly *Doctor Syn*). Canadian outline two-cylinder Pacific

Yorkshire Engine Co 2294/31

One of two similar machines, this locomotive was built officially by the Yorkshire Engine Co; it would perhaps be more correct to say that she was erected by them mainly from parts already made at New Romney and incorporated a complete boiler by Krauss of Munich. She was originally named *Doctor Syn*, after a famous fictional smuggling parson of Dymchurch, and was used consistently both up to and during the war. She was rebuilt at New Romney in 1947 and a year later, in September 1948, she was sent to Toronto for exhibition, being renamed *Winston Churchill* for the occasion. She was fitted with a new superheated standard boiler in 1959 at New Romney and in 1962 the Vanderbilt tender, very prone to leakages, was replaced by a handsome new conventional body on the original wheels and frames of No 10's tender. The body was built by Gower's of Bedford and did not incorporate a water scoop! Since then she has been in regular service but was converted to oil firing as an experiment in 1973 and was given a rebuild in 1973–4.

Livery originally was black with blued-steel boiler cladding. She was painted Wickham blue by the Army and ran like that in 1946. After the 1947 overhaul she became bright red and from 1962 on has been unlined black. She is now (1974) red.

No 10 *Dr Syn* (formerly *Black Prince*) Canadian outline two-cylinder Pacific
Yorkshire Engine Co 2295/31

The early history of No 10 is identical to that of No 9 except that because of a wheel-casting failure during re-tyring she acquired *Typhoon*'s wheels about 1936 and has retained them since. The extent of her war service is not known but she was rebuilt at New Romney during winter 1946–7 and in February 1949 was renamed *Dr Syn*, taking the name over from No 9. She was out of service from 1961 to 1964 but in that year emerged with a newly-rebodied tender, ex-No 9, and the last of the new superheated boilers from Gower's; the latter had been in store for nearly three years. She was used extensively in subsequent years, and during 1970–1 was stripped down, her frames and wheels being sent to Cushing Engineering of Rainham, Kent for rebuilding. She was reassembled during 1973 and put into service for the 1973 season.

Livery was originally as for No 9 but with red wheels and she remained black until 1953. She was then repainted GW green with maroon wheels, which lasted until the 1964 rebuild. From November 1964 she was black with white lettering and trim, this being changed to her present livery of black with red trim in 1973.

It is probably true to say that steam traction on the RH & D has always had a flavour all its own. This is partly a literal 'flavour', produced by the distinctive tang of the soft Kentish coal as the exhaust drifts back along the train at window height, and partly a matter of the wide variation in locomotive whistles. Captain Howey made something of a hobby out of collecting whistles on his travels and his successors have added one or two of their own. The current collection ranges from two of the original 'hooters', through American Crosby whistles to a chromium plated A4-pattern whistle with a history behind it. Howey was particularly taken with the deep toned Canadian type of whistle and acquired one for fitting to his Canadian Pacific. Sir Nigel Gresley, on a visit to Romney, was equally taken with the sound produced and proposed to fit similar ones to his, then new, A4 class Pacifics. Howey promptly presented him with the whistle and, in due course, received as a return gift the chromium plated facsimile, which currently adorns *Hurricane*. Latest whistle to join the line is one presented recently by Norman Sandley the well-known American enthusiast for the 15in gauge.

Steam Locomotive Dimensions (as built)

Dimension	1–3	4	5–6	7–8	9–10
Wheel arrangement	4–6–2	0–4–0	4–8–2	4–6–2	4–6–2
Cylinders (in)	$5\frac{1}{4} \times 8\frac{1}{2}$	$4\frac{9}{16} \times 6\frac{5}{16}$	$5\frac{1}{4} \times 8\frac{1}{2}$	$5\frac{1}{4} \times 8\frac{1}{2}$*	$5\frac{1}{4} \times 8\frac{1}{2}$
Coupled wheel dia (in)	$25\frac{1}{2}$	$15\frac{3}{4}$	$19\frac{1}{2}$	$25\frac{1}{2}$	$25\frac{1}{2}$
Coupled wheelbase (ft/in)	4/8	2/11$\frac{1}{2}$	5/6	4/8	4/8
Weight in WO—total (tons)	7·85	5·10	8·25	8·1	8·75
Water cap (gall)	150	135	150	150	300
Coal cap (lb)	670	330	670	670	840
Boiler pressure (lb/sq in)	180	171	180	180	200†

*Three-cylinder until mid-1930s.

†An error. Krauss recommended 14 atmospheres (171lb/sq in) but the boiler arrived set at 200lb/sq in and remained like that until about 1935 when a steam pipe collapsed. It was then rerated at 180lb/sq in.

Boilers: The differences between the original boilers and the new ones are shown below:

Dimensions	1–3,7/8	5/6	9/10	New
Boiler dia (in)	22⅝	22⅝	Tapered	22⅝
Length between tubeplates (ft/in)	7/6	8/1	7/0	7/3½
Evaporating surface (total) (sq ft)	124·25	133·20	95	115
Grate area (sq ft)	4·7	4·7	4·75	4·7
Superheating surface (sq ft)	11·0*	11·0*	8·9*	20

*Greenly's smokebox type.
NB Boilers for the 4–8–2s are standard with the rest but have a smokebox 7in longer.

PETROL LOCOMOTIVES

Theakston-Ford 4–4–0 20–22hp

This eight-wheeled vehicle was supplied by F. Theakston Ltd for the opening of the Dungeness extension in 1928. It was officially a 'Model T Ford as supplied to the R & ER' and probably had much the same origin—almost certainly being based on one of a pair of ex-WD Crewe Tractors acquired by the firm. Theakston's, however, had obviously taken to heart the lessons learnt from their earlier venture; the Ford car was put on a new chassis. Indeed, as built, it much resembled the R & ER's ICL No 1 in its final form, having a separate angle-iron frame with the Ford engine and chassis mounted thereon and driving the front axle of a rigid rear bogie via the original car back axle and a chain and sprocket reduction gear. The two rear rail axles were coupled by chains and the front of the frame was carried on a four-wheeled bogie with coil springing. The simple, panelled body also resembled ICL No 1 although it was rather more angular in appearance. It had a long low centre cab, with bench seat, and oblong 'bonnets' at each end. Electric headlamps were fitted for winter work, driven off the original car dynamo.

The unit suffered from the defects of its origin. It was rather slow in forward gear since the ratio of final drive was calculated to give 12½mph as the most efficient speed, and it had only one very low reverse gear since the original Model T gear-box was used. Nonetheless, it worked on light passenger trains until about 1934–5, especially in the off-season, but was withdrawn and broken up some time in the mid-1930s.

Rolls-Royce 4–4–OPM 45hp

The Theakston-Ford was useful enough for Captain Howey to want something better. In 1930–1 he therefore used his 1914 vintage Rolls-Royce Silver Ghost shooting brake as the basis of another petrol locomotive. The car chassis was extended at each end and complete with engine, radiator and bonnet was converted into a rail tractor at New Romney. The engine drove via a 'solid' crown wheel and pinion onto a rigid rear 'bogie', using the original gear-box. The 2ft 1½in diameter solid disc wheels were chain-coupled and the front of the frame was supported on a Gibbins bogie and fitted with a cow-catcher. A match-boarded cab and rear locker were mounted on this frame behind the car bonnet and two large headlights were provided for working after dark. It ran for twelve months with the original engine which was then replaced by a six-cylinder OHV 45hp engine from a Rolls ambulance. The resulting machine was quite successful and very fast in forward gear; it is recorded that on one occasion with a light load of four Claytons, Captain Howey attained the speed of 60·2mph.

By the end of the war, the original body was just about worn out and a new and rather 'flashy' metal body was fabricated in 1946. The following year a Fordson 20hp lorry engine replaced the Rolls one and the locomotive was used to operate early and late trains. Soon afterwards it was withdrawn and the front bogie was 'borrowed' for *Northern Chief*'s tender. The remainder lingered on in the shed until the end of 1961 when it was broken up (week ending 16 December 1961).

JAP Scooter

About 1929 Captain Howey had constructed at New Romney a small 'scooter' which he used as personal transport. It consisted of a simple rectangular wooden frame with small (10½in) wheels in sprung axle boxes. It was powered by a very elegant British-built 6hp 'V' twin motor cycle engine which had been a show engine on the stand of J. A. Prestwich at the Olympia exhibition (hence the 'J. A. P.'). The machine had a wooden box-well between the frames and the driver sat virtually on top of the main frames with his feet in this well. A vertical board partition gave him some protection from wind and engine oil and also acted as a dashboard on which was mounted rudimentary instrumentation, the oil tank and a two-gallon petrol tank. A very weak handbrake provided the only stopping power and starting was accomplished by pushing until the engine fired and then jumping nimbly aboard as the machine accelerated away. Drive was by the then current motor-cycle method of rubber belts. The scooter was usually driven 'solo' but could—and at times did—transport up to four people, two facing forward, the other two back to back with them with their legs perched precariously on the rear 'buffer beam'. The machine certainly survived the war but was broken up soon after. It was in its prime the fastest piece of motive power on the railway and incorporated a screw jack and turning plate that enabled it to be turned at any point on the line.

The WD Scooter 4-WPM 7hp

The War Department technicians, for their own use, originally built a four-wheeled scooter, constructed on a wagon frame about 1929 and powered by a 7hp Austin Seven engine. It is said to have been rather similar to the railway's scooter but more massive and much slower; its progress was the subject of many jokes. The machine survived into the early 1960s but disappeared when the machine described below was built. In its latter years it acquired the radiator off the former Rolls tractor.

The RH & D Scooter 4-WPM 1,000cc

In 1962 the railway constructed a new scooter for permanent way work using the wheels and axles from one of its predecessors. It was erected—there is no other word—on a four-wheeled well frame of the post war (Clifford Edwards) batch and incorporated an Austin Seven engine and the radiator from the old Rolls. It is now mildly peculiar in appearance, resembling nothing so much as several modified packing cases neatly put together and painted dull black, the radiator being concealed within the body shell. Engine changes were made in 1967 and again in 1971. The machine must now be nearing the end of its days but has been a very useful unit in its time.

No 4 Simplex 4-WPM 20hp

In 1947, the company acquired a standard 20hp plate framed Simplex petrol tractor from Eaton Hall. This was a straightforward descendant of the famous 'Simplex' tractors used in World War I, and was composed basically of a four-wheeled steel frame on which was mounted a two-cylinder petrol engine, a radiator and a driver's cab. Final drive was by the patent Dixon-Abbott gear-box to chains and sprockets. This tractor was built for 15in gauge, having been supplied to the Duke of Westminster's estate railway in 1938 and was MR 7059/38. It was passed to the associated Romney Marsh Ballast Co and when rail traffic in ballast ceased in 1951, it was taken back into railway stock and numbered 4. Its original cab was cut down on arrival to suit the RH & D loading gauge and it is painted green. It was converted to diesel at New Romney in 1967 and was re-engined and re-wheeled in 1972.

A second, similar Simplex tractor operated on the railway about 1962–4 in connection with a major drainage scheme. This was the property of the contractors and was a standard 2ft gauge machine converted simply by pressing wheels inwards on their axles. Except that it fouled certain structures unless turned on a turntable, this tractor was quite adequate but was removed on completion of the contract.

LOCOMOTIVES NEVER BUILT

At various times locomotives proposed for use on the RH & DR have been designed but for varying reasons have never been built. A very brief summary of these is given below:

1   The two 'English' type Pacifics ordered from Davey Paxman in 1928. These were to have been exactly as *Green Goddess* but were discontinued in favour of the CPRs. It is possible that some of their castings were utilised for the latter.

2   A 4–6–2 'Princess Royal' LMS-type Pacific. This was ordered by Captain Howey about 1936 and various parts, including the main frames, were actually started. The locomotive was being built by H. C. S. Bullock of Farnborough and work stopped on his untimely death in 1937. The parts already made were brought to New Romney and the frames were still (1973) in the stores there. Scale was to have been 1:3 as with all the other machines.

3   After the war, with the prospect of a large ballast traffic, Howey commissioned Mr H. Holcroft of the Southern Railway CME's department to design a completely new mixed-traffic locomotive. This was to be an entirely freelance machine and full drawings were prepared for a neat 2–8–2 of rather plain, English, appearance;

it was not, as reputed, similar to an unstreamlined P2. The locomotive was never built, Howey hankering after something more
exotic—which led to the following further design studies. None
of these got further than drawings.

4   A three-cylinder 4–8–4 by H. Holcroft; outline drawings of this
    British type locomotive only were completed, in 1948.
5   A massive American style six-cylinder Duplex drive 4–4–4–4
    designed at Captain Howey's request by Ian Hunter of Glossop
    about 1947. The project was abandoned in favour of:
6   A three-cylinder American 4–8–4 Niagara type machine also
    designed by Mr Hunter. It was reputedly for this machine that
    the 40ft turntable was put in at Hythe.

In retrospect one wonders just how serious most of these projects
were. Certainly by 1951 it was clear that freight traffic would once
more be non-existent and that the existing stud was quite capable
of handling the passenger traffic. Certainly at one period shortly after
the war there was also talk of a Bulleid-type Pacific but this appears
to have come to nothing; possibly the Holcroft 2–8–2 was put forward
as being more suitable.

CHAPTER 9

Rolling Stock

By this point in the book, the reader will be accepting as inevitable the cry that nothing is certain—as in all other aspects of the RH & D it is difficult to find out exactly what the rolling stock position was in early years; in this case confusion is made even more complicated by the ease with which 15in gauge vehicles can be rebuilt, cannibalised, or just plain hacked about. Thus a 1972-built coach body on a 1935 vintage (elongated) frame may well have bogies that started life under an articulated (ex-four wheel) coach in 1930. Quite clearly too, after its first year or so the company paid very little attention to the annual Board of Trade returns—a concern that can cover the scrapping of over 60 vehicles and their replacement by 56 bogie coaches as 'no change—30 scrapped, 30 new' is not to be trusted on matters of detail! There is, therefore, plenty for any cognoscenti to argue about.

PRE-WAR COACHES

1 *Original coaching stock*
The coaching stock provided for the opening, in 1927, consisted of four-wheeled semi-open vehicles, designed by Henry Greenly himself. Greenly went to great trouble to examine the problems posed by the RH & D, in particular the need for a long wheelbase and a low centre of gravity to counteract the effect of strong winds blowing over the exposed marsh. He and his son Kenneth even went to the lengths of building a mock-up and subjecting it to tests, using blocks and suspended weights to find out what force was needed to overturn the vehicle. The result was a steel girder underframe in the form of a partial-well; that is to say the main frame was very low slung but angled up at each end to accomodate a pair of wheels and their axle mounted rigidly in the frame. The headstocks and buffer-beam were fitted directly to the end of this angle piece and on this frame a two-

compartment wooden body was mounted. It was framed and panelled in hardwood, and open above the waist but had glassed end screens and a glassed partition between the two 'compartments'. The seats were upholstered in brown rexine with matching back cushions and the roof was of plywood sheathed with aluminium. The bodies were supplied complete, except for minor fittings, by Martin Walter's of Folkstone and were assembled at New Romney onto frames and wheels supplied by Francis Theakston Ltd. A special miniaturised vacuum brake equipment was designed and built by the Vacuum Brake Company, and this was also added at New Romney by Jackson, Rigby Ltd who fabricated in addition such items as the buffing gear, drawbars, etc.

The result was a very stable vehicle but one which had all the disadvantages of a model-engineering approach. The plain, oil-lubricated journals were susceptible to hot-boxes and their rigidity gave rise to a hunting motion at speed; the open sides, while excellent for stability, proved rather chilly for the passengers. On the credit side, the vehicles were well made and so bottom-heavy that if turned on their sides for maintenance they had to be tied down if they were not to rock upright again immediately.

Initially, it would appear that 60 coaches and two brake/luggage vans were ordered, the van bodies being built by Jackson, Rigby's on normal steel underframes. The first annual stock return for 1927, however, shows 57 coaches and 5 brake vans and this is confirmed by contemporary notes that extra vans were 'built'—or rather con-verted—at New Romney before the opening. It was the intention to include a brake van in each train and the only available photograph of one shows it as having the standard pattern body but with only one door each side and four small side windows. The vans were fitted with brake valves and gauges; all coaches were piped but only half had brakes so they were quickly close-coupled in pairs to avoid complications. Livery was a darkish green with grey or white roofs and the letters *RH & DR* along the sides. Coaches sported a number centrally on each side at waist level, and the vans were clearly lettered 'Guard's Van' in the same place.

Six were delivered in time for the Duke of York's visit in August 1926 and the remainder were available for the opening. Even so, they proved insufficient in face of the rising traffic and the railway promptly announced its intention of building 60 more.

The second batch is something of a mystery since the underframes appear identical but were not ordered from Theakston's—on the other hand Theakstons were mainly agents and probably 'bought-in' the frames they did supply. Certainly, once again the major components were built elsewhere and put together at New Romney with locally fabricated minor fittings. The bodies were not quite identical having sheet iron roofs and slightly wider roof pillars with a half-round beading along the coach sides at waist-level. The seats were boarded and were provided with horsehair-filled loose cushions initially though from photographic evidence they appear to have been fitted with upholstered seat backs at a later date. From the start these vehicles were painted in the 'new' livery of brown and yellowish cream—'not *quite* Great Western' as one person put it—and the earlier batch were repainted in these colours quite quickly. From notes and contemporary records it appears that while 60 were ordered and built only 55 went into service, five being sold new to a showman at Porthcawl. This is partly confirmed by the 1928 stock returns which show an increase of 63—this would be eight Clayton bogies (qv) and 55 four-wheelers.

The second batch were announced as 'summer-coaches' but even for summer work the completely open sides proved inconveniently draughty. Experiments were initially made with flexible, transparent mica side screens that pegged into the roof cantrails and waist. These can be seen in a number of photographs and it is possible they were installed for the 1927–8 winter service. They were not successful, having a tendency to blow out and float away, so it was decided to turn all coaches into semi enclosed stock. This was done by fitting four small windows on each side, leaving the upper part of the door openings clear. All vehicles were so converted by about 1931, the earlier ones appearing in the chocolate and cream livery. Complete enclosure was not needed since Clayton bogie coaches (qv) had been delivered for winter service.

Even in their modified state the four-wheeled coaches were not really satisfactory and it was therefore decided to articulate them in sets to try to improve the ride and reduce drag. The railway had 'discovered' the Gibbins equalised bogie in 1930 and had rebogied its Clayton coaches early that year. A further 16 bogies were delivered in May for articulation purposes, apparently as an experiment and 90 more of the same type were delivered, all from Gloucester Carriage & Wagon Co in the autumn.

Once more uncertainty descends. According to staff, only five-

and nine-car sets (four and eight bogies respectively) were built at New Romney but various visitors during the 1930s have recorded the presence of triplets (or at least of odd formations such as eight-car trains that would imply the presence of triplet sets). It is possible by means of devious calculations to show that the result must have been so many of each; indeed the author has been presented with no less than three estimates, each widely different, and has had no trouble in concocting a couple more to give different results again. Add the facts that no one is certain whether all coaches were converted and that at least 11 were sold out of service (five to Porthcawl, six with *The Bug*) and no certain result can be assured. Suffice to say that the majority were certainly quins or nontuplets. The articulation involved use of massive linking pieces with pivot holes into which pivots under the headstocks fitted; the end coaches of a set retained their outer wheels and axles. It appears to have improved the ride to some degree but the coaches were still unsatisfactory and were largely replaced during 1934–5 by new bogie vehicles. A great many were scrapped during 1935 as some 62 of the bogies were required for use under the new bogie saloons and most of the remainder followed in 1936 when track through Littlestone tunnels was packed up to obviate flooding. The resulting loading gauge was insufficient for the articulated sets and only a few—probably about 30 coaches in all—were retained for short workings over the New Romney–Hythe section. At least some of these, probably three quint-sets, were converted into an emergency reserve of open coaches for the 1938 season by simply removing the roof and side windows, and sawing off the ends at seat-back level. These few remaining sets had their bodies stripped off during the war and were used, with other vehicles, for transporting PLUTO pipeline (see page 65). Three frame-sets survived the war in runnable form but only one saw further passenger-service, a botched four-underframe set on two Gibbins and one Hudson bogie. During a stock crisis in 1947 this was fitted with a simple open bodywork having doorless entrances and was later fitted with mesh 'roofs'. It ran as a set until about 1959, for some time at least as a three car unit, and was then withdrawn and dumped beside the up line at New Romney. It was immediately robbed of its bogies which were urgently needed elsewhere and thereafter gradually fell to pieces. With its passing ended the saga of the four-wheelers, although the odd coach body may well lie around on the marsh; they were given away in 1935–6 to anyone who wanted them.

Dimensions of the original vehicles were: length over headstocks 10ft 0¼in, width 3ft 4in, height 6ft. They tared: 17cwt.

2 The 'Clayton' Pullmans

Fortunately there is no doubt about these eight bogie vehicles. Henry Greenly had recognised in August 1927 that closed coaches would be needed for the winter traffic and the contract was placed that autumn with the Clayton Wagon Co through Theakston's. The coaches were three-compartment, 12-seaters with sprung upholstered seats, steam heating, electric lighting and, as the railway proudly pointed out, real photographs on the compartment bulkheads. The handsome, semi-elliptical roofed coach-built bodies were on steel well-frames, the space above each bogie in each coach being utilised for luggage and for the batteries supplying electricity for lighting. They were painted in the now standard chocolate and cream having RH & D transfers in gold, shaded blue, and were generally much admired. Only the *Railway Magazine* said, rather carpingly, that there seemed to be a great deal of wasted space. They were rebogied with Gibbins bogies in 1930.

Until 1935 these 'Pullmans' were the pride of the line but as the new saloons came into service they were relegated to less important work. In 1936, with the reduction in loading gauge, they were cut down to 5ft 3in in height, a fairly drastic operation involving new roofs, the removal of lighting, and some surgery to body uprights and window glasses. They thus assumed their present form.

The 'Claytons' nevertheless lasted well. They were used regularly by the Army during the war, being the only coaching stock vehicles to be given Army running numbers (110–17) which they still carried in 1973. The steam heating was removed after the war and livery was changed first to blue and cream and thence to green and cream while various minor rebuildings and upholsterings have taken place over the years. In 1973 all were in poor condition, three of the eight being virtually withdrawn. The railway's coaching stock plan calls for several to be rebuilt to provide 1st class accomodation for which there is a demand, and the first rebuilds, probably to 'standard' outline may be in service by the time this book appears. Dimensions as new were similar to the four-wheelers except for the length (20ft). Bogie wheelbase was 2ft.

Page 125 (top) *Greenly 4–8–2 nameless in 1927;* (centre) *4–6–2 No 9,* Winston Churchill, *with her original Vanderbilt tender, in 1959;* (below) *A collection of visitors: L to R* Tracy Jo (2–6–2P); Prince Charles *(4–6–2, ¼-scale); line of:* Cagney *4–4–0;* Dutch *0–4–0; a Romney Pacific*

Page 126 (top) *0–4–0TT No 4, The Bug; (centre) The Rolls-Royce tractor, Howey 'up', shunting 1935 saloons at Hythe. It is in post-1947 form; (left) The current (1973) scooter coupled to the surviving Jackson Rigby bogie wagon*

3 *The 'Hudson–Hythe' saloons*

If the Claytons were thought to contain wasted space, the next set of coaches was positively prodigal of room. In 1934 Captain Howey ordered from Robert Hudson Ltd 16ft long well-chassis for no less than 54 modern bogie coaches and two bogie vans, with the intention of completely re-equipping the railway. The bodies for these vehicles were built by the Hythe Cabinet and Joinery Works. They were spacious saloon bodies and their comfort was superlative—hence the later epithet 'Pullman-plus' which was unofficial and never liked by the railway, but which did achieve some popularity in books. Each coach seated eight people on large, interior sprung seats upholstered in moquette and arranged in two 'compartments'. There was no interior partition so that large central windows could be installed to improve the passenger's view, wide shelves at each end provided luggage space and the wood-framed, metal-clad, bodies incorporated several features of contemporary motor car design such as the trim, door handles and the wind-down door windows. These coaches were painted a darkish green and cream and were either piped or equipped with vacuum brakes in a ratio of half and half. The brake cylinder was sited between the central pair of seats. They had no running numbers initially but nonetheless cryptic number groups such as C/11/3 appeared on coach-ends to puzzle enthusiasts. This was because the 'Romney' had brought off quite a coup, persuading Pinchin Johnson, paint manufacturers, to paint everything on the line at their own cost in return for which the railway acted as a mobile weathering laboratory; the curious numbers were paint specifications and it is said that in the right light conditions the differing surface textures along an RH & D train were fascinating to watch! At a later date some coaches at least received running numbers prefixed by the letter A (eg A2).

At least a few coaches were immediately fitted with electric light for late evening, and winter-working, a Kohler generating set being installed in one of the vans to provide power; and in 1938, ten of these were painted blue and made into a permanent rake for use on the Blue Train introduced that year. A number of saloons was used by the Army during the war and some were wrecked, either by enemy action or our own troops. The frames were reused and by 1955–6 when a stock numbering scheme was completed only 29 remained in working order; the remainder had been rebuilt in some way. The surviving originals continued in use during the late 1950s and early

H

1960s, their numbers slowly diminishing until by late 1965 only two were in service in their original form while another seven were stored in poor condition. These were all rebuilt during the following winters and the subsequent history of their frames will be found under '16ft rebuilds'. Dimensions were: length over headstocks: 16ft, width 3ft 4in, height 5ft 7in. The first 25 were fitted with Hudson bogies and the remainder with Gibbins bogies 'recovered' from scrapped articulated sets.

POST-WAR REBUILDS

Up to 1939, the RH & D was at least fairly consistent in its stock; since 1945 the position has become much more complicated with some frames carrying two or three bodies in succession while some are now being elongated with new centre sections. The position is summarised below, so far as possible in chronological order.

1 Ex-hopper wagons

Following the war five chassis remained available out of the six formerly carrying hopper wagon bodies (see page 142). These five 22ft long frames were stripped of their wagon bodies in 1947 and during 1947–8 were fitted with new ply-panelled coach bodies by Kent & Sussex Woodcraft Ltd of Ashford. These were classed as 'Pullmans', being painted in the Pullman livery of umber and cream with appropriate lettering, and were designed as a set; the three centre coaches were 20-seaters, while each outer coach had one end sloped in imitation of the Southern Railway 'beaver-tail' cars, and seated only 18. The bodies were no less than 4ft wide—very broad for the 15in gauge—and had a single door centrally placed in each side; access to seats was by a centre gangway. RH & D vacuum pipes and couplers were fitted at this time.

Initially the vehicles were run as individual units, being delivered at various times in late 1947 and early 1948 but in winter 1949–50 they were all equipped with brakes and were then marshalled as a set with the Eaton parcels van (see page 146) in the middle. The vehicles looked very smart when new but their wooden bodies had little rigidity and deteriorated rapidly. In the winter of 1953–4 they were numbered 300–4 and painted in a temporary livery of drab green, a colour also applied to some of the older saloon stock about that time. The rapidly decaying bodies were scrapped and replaced in time for the 1955 season by green and cream semi-open bodies with transverse seating built at New Romney. The angular bodywork somewhat recalled the original four-wheelers with straight wooden sides, and double windows between five entrances on each side. The three centre 'compartments' had externally mounted sliding doors, the small end compartments over each bogie having doorless entrances. Seats were fitted with Dunlopillo cushions covered in Rexine.

The doors were not entirely successful and were removed in 1965–6 under the Collins regime. The coaches then ran as semi-opens until 1971–4 when they were successively rebodied in the new 'standard' style with beading 'panels' and larger windows to give maximum visibility. They are now chocolate and cream with grey roofs and grey interiors. Current dimensions are: length over headstocks 22ft, width 3ft 6in, height 5ft 4in.

2 Eaton Hall stock
Immediately after the war, passenger stock was in short supply and, in desperation, Captain Howey purchased all remaining vehicles of the Duke of Westminster's Eaton Railway. These included, besides various goods vehicles (see page 146), three passenger coaches built over 50 years before by Sir Arthur Heywood to his maximum loading gauge principles. They were consequently too tall for the RH & D and, after arrival, were soon cut down as the Claytons had been; the operation, however was a little simpler and they retained their original roofs. All are still in existence.

(i) *Closed coach*: Youngest of the three, this was a standard pattern Heywood 16-seater delivered to Eaton Hall about 1904. As delivered, and as it arrived at New Romney, it had three elegantly equipped 'compartments' with blue rep upholstery and blue window curtains; there were no internal bulkheads since light at night was provided by a carriage lamp at each end, mounted externally and shining through a round porthole in each end bulkhead. The design was slightly improved over Heywood's earlier vehicles, having two large windows between each door, and the vehicle was substantially built in varnished teak; like all his other coaches no space was wasted, the two 'outside passengers' being accommodated in outward facing seats at each end over the bogies and protected by tubular handrails. The bogies were Heywood's own short-wheelbase affairs with rubber 'springing'. This coach was soon stripped of its finery and cut down to enable it to pass Littlestone tunnels, acquiring short roof extensions over the end seats about 1960.

(ii) *Open Coach*: Part of the original Eaton Hall equipment this was a standard Heywood vehicle dating from 1896 and seating sixteen passengers in the same fashion as the closed coach. As built it had buttoned leather loose cushions but these do not appear to have survived at New Romney. There it eventually acquired first a mesh roof and then a hardboard roof to protect passengers against hitting their heads on bridges but was not otherwise altered.

(iii) *Brake Van*: Again part of the original Eaton Hall equipment this vehicle was a normal Heywood 14ft brake van with a central four-seat van compartment entered by sliding doors in each side, and the usual outside seats at each end. Like the closed coach it was cut down at New Romney on arrival and fitted to carry six passengers internally together with four outside; about 1960 these were given protecting roof extensions. Small windows were cut in the sides and doors but visibility for passengers was never good.

All these vehicles ran for some time on their original bogies which, while no doubt satisfactory for estate work, were rather crude for RH & D work and speeds. Since no one bothered to replace the perished rubber blocks their noise and ride approximated to that of a rather noisy tramcar—or so it is said—and they were soon refitted with Gibbins bogies and Marillier couplings; the closed coach also lost its doors which were proving rather vulnerable. In 1952–3 all three vehicles were numbered into stock, the closed coach first receiving the number 8 (in error) and then 699 (classed as a semi-open), the open becoming 409 and the brake van 207 (later 698). Nos 699 and 409 are still—1973—in active service in green and cream but 698 is withdrawn in poor condition. All are scheduled for restoration. Dimensions are: length over headstocks 13ft 1in (van), width 3ft 6in, height (orig) 6ft.

3 'Gower' coaches

In 1962 the first entirely new coach frames for almost thirty years were supplied to the railway. These are 20ft long steel well frames built by Gowers of Bedford for which new bogies were provided; six were supplied in 1962 and two more in 1966. The original six were fitted at New Romney with wooden bodies built by a local firm, Vidler's of Dymchurch. The bow sided bodies are reminiscent of the 1934 saloons but have slightly smaller windows with radiused ends and seat sixteen in three 'compartments'; they are fitted with internally sliding doors and are numbered 800–5. The two other frames, now 806–7, remained in store for some years until fitted in 1968 with rather more angular bodies built by Sullivan at New Romney. The seating arrangement is the same and illustrates the problems of the RH & D loading gauge since the two seats at each end are really suitable only for children; they have to be reached by scrambling over a narrow gap in the next two seat-backs. The vehicles were painted green and cream when new and either fitted (800/2/3/5) or piped (801/4/6/7) for vacuum brakes. At the time of writing all except 805 are running in original condition. 805 was rebuilt with a standard body incorporating roof air scoops in 1971 and the rest are scheduled for reconstruction in due course. Dimensions (original series) are: length 19ft 8in, width 3ft 10in, height 5ft 3in.

4 The Jumping Jacks

About 1951, four well frames of the 1947 batch (qv) were provided with 4ft wide, open, two-compartment bodies. They were converted to semi-brake vans for the 1953 season by building a crude 'hut' over one compartment and numbered 502–5. One was blown over at half-mile curve in 1954 after which they were condemned as unsafe and again rebuilt as open coaches, receiving the numbers 701–4. No 702 was stripped to form the basis of a scooter in 1962, the others being out of use by 1964 and later scrapped. They gave a very harsh ride owing to the coil springs fitted, and were unofficially known as the *Jumping Jacks*.

5 Rebuilds of the 1934 saloons

Not unnaturally the majority of the railway's coaches are rebuilds of the 1934 stock. The massive well frames and their bogies have easily outlasted the original bodywork and are far too valuable to scrap. At the same time their design with its lavish provision for eight passengers but great inconvenience for any more has proved a considerable handicap to the railway; surprisingly only recently has the obvious step been taken of dismantling the frames and inserting new lengthened centre portions to allow for greater seating capacity. The task is comparatively easy since the wells are formed by massive cast 'knees' at each end which simply join the bogie-mounts to the central girders; although this will not entirely obviate waste of space over the bogies it will considerably reduce it elsewhere. As mentioned, however, this is a recent innovation; up to 1971 all rebuilding of the 1934 stock was carried out on the original frames and usually over a period. In the following notes the dates given are for the majority of each 'batch' and the running numbers given are those resulting from Driver Hobbs's renumbering scheme of 1953–5; although the coaches did not carry a clear sequence of numbers before that, they will be used here for convenience.

(i) *Open coaches*: In 1946 it was found that a considerable number of the original saloons were beyond repair—either damaged by enemy action or dismantled by the Army. There was an urgent need to provide passenger stock and so fifteen open coaches, later known as the 4XX series, were constructed at New Romney in 1947–8. They were of two distinct varieties, Nos 401/2/4/8/11 being less robust than the others; the reason appears to be that the work was entrusted to two men, each being responsible for turning out complete coach bodies to a general specification but his own detailed design. All were 16 seaters using hardwood seats and after a few seasons were fitted with wire mesh 'roofs' to stop passengers bumping their heads against bridges. These roofs were built almost to the limits of the loading gauge and, after one or two disastrous occasions when they scraped the tunnel roofs, bringing down showers of soot on the occupants, were replaced by painted hardboard. The vehicles were all either fitted or piped, had doorless entrances and were painted plain green. Final running numbers ran from 400 to 416 with two exceptions—409 was allocated to the Heywood open coach and 414 to the post-war articulated set. In 1971 three, Nos 402/6/11, were rebodied in a style matching the new standard closed coaches and since then Nos 405 and 415 have been withdrawn from service as part of the reconstruction programme. It is intended to retain 15 open coaches in stock, however, since they provide maximum seating capacity for a 16ft frame and are very useful at peak periods. Consequently more rebuilds will appear in due course. Dimensions are: length over headstocks 16ft, width 3ft 6in, height 5ft 3in.

(ii) *Observation cars*: Two notable conversions in 1946–7 were observation cars called *Pluto* and *Martello* with bodies by Kent and Sussex Woodcraft. These bodies were semi-streamlined with sloping ends and a central door in each side, and seated eight people all facing towards the centre; the end bench seats were reached by a 'gangway' between bucket seats, the vehicles being 4ft wide to allow for this. Livery was blue and cream with a garter on each door bearing the words 'Observation Car RH & DR' and the car's name. Roofboards proclaimed 'The Bluecoaster Limited' and it was intended that at stations, observation car passengers would be served refreshments at their seats; this was not done in practice. Both cars were ex-saloons, *Pluto* being numbered P26 and *Martello* P23; the former was rebuilt as an ordinary coach in 1956 but *Martello* survived until the 1966 rebuilding (qv).

(iii) *The 'Queen Anne' coaches*: Next batch to be rebuilt was the seven coaches reconstructed by carpenter Hooper at New Romney in 1953–4 as 12-seaters. Just why they were given this sobriquet is not clear but they were fairly stately looking vehicles with four-square angular bodies and four 'compartments'. The centre ones had no doors or dividing partition but were cut off from the small two-seat compartments over each bogie. They were numbered in the 6XX series from new and 601–2 were ordinary 12-seaters. Following the derailment of a light brake van in 1954, however, the remainder 600/3–6 were fitted with a brake valve under the seat in one end compartment so that they could be used as vans and were classed as 10-seaters. These compartments were provided with lockable inward-opening doors and the guard carried a special key which unlocked the door and also operated the train brakes via a brake valve reached by raising a brass flap in the seat. The only other item of note was that 604 was specially fitted with a massive brass porthole at each end in imitation of the Heywood closed coach which Howey much admired. Unlike the Heywood portholes, however, these served no useful purpose. These coaches, latterly in green and cream, soon had the guard's compartment doors removed and have for some years been used as 12-seaters. All were in poor condition by 1973 and by the time this book appears the bodies are likely to have been scrapped. Dimensions were: length over headstocks 16ft, width 3ft 5in, height 5ft 2in.

(iv) *The '1956' saloons*: For the 1956 Blue Train, Hooper built eight 8-seater saloon bodies generally similar to the 'Queen Annes'. These were angular vehicles with board seats and hinged doors with wind-down windows. They incorporated various fittings from their predecessors and had all the same problems—such as wasted space—but without their comfort. They did, however, make a standard rake of quite pleasing appearance and were used regularly for the named train—latterly the Marshlander and then once more the Blue Train—for over a decade. They were initially painted blue and cream, latterly green and cream, and the running numbers were 1, 5, 17, 24/6/7/9, 33. It is possible that No 13, discussed in detail below, joined them in 1957. It may be noted that No 1 was built on a frame that had lain derelict for some years. All except 13 survived into the 1970s but No 33 was rebodied in 1971, serving as a prototype for the new standard style. Dimensions were: length 16ft, width 3ft 5in, height 5ft 2½in.

(v) *The '1962' saloons*: During the years 1961–3 a carpenter named Everest was employed by the railway in succession to Hooper. He first rebuilt Nos 14 and 32 during 1961 in a distinctive style unlike that of any other vehicles on the railway. The coaches were 12-seaters having two main 'compartments' with internally fitted sliding doors and two small end compartments over the bogies with hinged doors. There were no internal partitions and the windows were very shallow with deeply radiused ends. Slatted seats were fitted. Both these vehicles survived in service in 1973.

During the winter of 1961–2 and the following season Everest also rebodied Nos 11, 13, 16, 25 and 30. By this time he was a fairly sick man and the rebuilding, to a fairly handsome design that was perpetuated by his successors, incorporated portions of the old saloons including the roofs and some of the framing. The coaches thus resembled their predecessors in general appearance, having two main 'compartments' with sliding doors and large windows. They were 12-seaters, access to the end seats being by a gap in the seats directly in front. The rebodying of these vehicles was more of a major rebuild than a completely new body and their lives were short. Only 11 and 16 remained in service in this form in 1973.

(vi) *The Vidler saloons*: Since the railway was not able to replace coaches quickly enough using only its own labour, a local firm, Vidler's of Dymchurch, was commissioned to make some bodies. Initially they built new bodies for the 8XX series (qv) but during 1963 and 1964 they also rebodied Nos 9, 18, 22 (in 1963) and Nos

12, 20, 28 (during the 1964 season). The general body style followed
that of Everest and the coaches were similarly 12-seaters with slatted
seats and two sliding doors a side; they can be recognised in photographs by their planked ends. All were still in service in 1973.

In 1964 Mr Vidler retired from the business but one of his former
employees, a Mr Grimaldi, was employed by the railway to rebody
three further coaches in a similar style. These, completed during the
1965 season, were Nos 10, 15 and 19. All were still in service in 1973
but much patched and generally in bad condition. Indeed the railway
appears to have built at minimum cost during the years 1961–5
and the vehicles built then have deteriorated rapidly; in some cases
the amount of 'bodging' required to keep them in service has almost
concealed their origin.

(vii) *The Sullivan saloons*: Fortunately in the summer of 1965 the
railway discovered the firm of Geo. Sullivan & Co of Lydd. Sullivan
obviously had a very clear idea of how to build a railway coach and
while sticking fairly closely to the existing design he adapted it for
series production. Indeed the major components, including the
complete sides and ends, were fabricated at Lydd and brought
complete to New Romney for assembly into existing frames. He also,
after several experiments, devised an effective method of roof
construction by stretching heavy calico over the roof timbers and
soaking it liberally with paint. This avoided the unsightly and largely
ineffective metal hoops common to all previous construction and has
proved surprisingly durable. In all, eleven vehicles, Nos 2, 3, 4, 6, 7,
8, 13, 21, 23, 25 and 31 were rebodied in this way between 1965 and
1967. Of these it will be noted that 13, 25 and 30 had previously
been rebuilt by Everest. As previously the coaches are 12-seaters with
slatted seats and internally fitted sliding doors; a few have now been
fitted with cushioned seats and the class is likely to be the last pre-
consortium type of coach to survive.

(viii) *No 13*: This coach is something of a problem, its recent history
being somewhat obscure. The railway's carriage and wagon books
record it as being rebuilt by Hooper in 1957 and it is noted as a 'new
saloon' up to 1960, after which it is noted as 'old' for the next two
years. It is recorded as having been rebuilt by Everest in 1962–3 and
was noted in a stock census in 1964 as being of 1956 pattern. It was
certainly rebodied by Sullivan in 1966–7 under the circumstances

described below. The most likely truth is that it was not part of the 1956 scheme, but suffered enough damage in some minor incident to be heavily rebuilt by Everest using similar parts and was shaky enough to be condemned when a particularly splendid coach was wanted. This happened in 1966-7 when Mr Collins, the then owner, decided he wanted a super saloon. No 13 was chosen, her frame being fitted with a standard Sullivan body shell quite sumptuously furnished in wood veneers and light blue leathercloth. To perpetuate the memory of the royal visit in 1957, the brass plaques formerly fitted to No 10 were transferred to this vehicle which also received No 10's bogies. It was painted first blue and cream and then (1972) brown and cream and is available for special charter. Dimensions are, as for all Sullivan's coaches, length 16ft, width 3ft 10in, height 5ft 2in.

(ix) *'Standard' coaches*: Experiments in 1970-1 resulted in a new body style for coach rebuilds, designed to provide homogeneous rakes of stock. This, tried out in prototype form on former saloon 33, is straight sided with maximum window area and with beaded 'panelling' below the waist line. As in previous rebuilds the end seats are reached by scrambling between two others but these latter have been designed as bucket seats to give maximum space. All seats are upholstered in leathercloth-covered foam rubber and the sliding doors are designed to jog closed if left open. The same pattern was applied to Vidler saloon 805 and since the 1972 takeover a completely new body using the same style has been developed.

These new coaches, numbered in the 5X series, incorporate various parts of old vehicles but are in reality new vehicles and will be referred to as such. They are based on reconditioned end-portions from 16ft chassis with a new, longer centre section bringing chassis length up to 23ft 4½in. Completely rebuilt Hudson or Gibbins bogies are fitted, equipped with heavy duty springs to take the extra weight. The bodies, built in hardwood, are 20-seaters and are currently finished in an attractive varnished livery with the railway crest on each side. A total of thirty is planned. Dimensions are: length 24ft, width 3ft 6in, height 5ft 3in.

ROLLING STOCK REGISTER

The ease with which 15in gauge rolling stock is modified makes it very difficult to produce an accurate record of coaching stock—which has in any case only been documented at all since the mid-1950s. The detailed list below refers to the position as at 31 August 1973 and requires some explanation.

(i) The coach numbers given are those at the completion of Driver Hobbs's renumbering scheme and were in existence by November 1955 at which time thirty three Hudson–Hythe frames still bore bodies classed as saloons. By January 1957 these included eight rebodied frames and one observation car, leaving twenty four of the old coaches in use. Numbers in brackets after these coaches show the numbers carried prior to 1955.

(ii) Rebodying is a difficult term to define. Coaches were reconstructed one after another in most cases so that no exact dates can be given; references in the carriage and wagon books date the year of rebuilding only and there appears to have been slow but steady work going on all round the year. In a few cases a 'rebodying' may have been in the nature of a heavy rebuild and in many cases vehicles have subsequently been patched to various extents—ranging from a new panel to a complete coach side! This may well have happened several times to the same coach.

(iii) Because of the drastic changes, the 5X series are included as new coaches and the note 'scrapped' against various vehicles indicates that the frame has been withdrawn: it is likely that components find their way into new vehicles but not always are they identifiable.

Passenger Rolling Stock as at 31 August 1972
(i) *16ft saloons* (see notes at end of table)

Running No		date	maker	Rebodyings seats type	date	maker
1	(31)	1956	RH & D/Hooper	8 CHD		
2	(C/11/3)	1967	RH & D/Sullivan	12 CSD		
3	(32)	1967	RH & D/Sullivan	12 CSD		
4	(12)	1967	RH & D/Sullivan	12 CSD		
5	(15)	1956	RH & D/Hooper	8 CHD		
6	(38)	1965	RH & D/Sullivan	12 CSD		
7	(A5)	1965	RH & D/Sullivan	12/CSD		
8	(14)	1966	RH & D/Sullivan	12 CSD		
9	(11)	1963	Vidler	12 CSD		
10	(A1)	1965	RH & D/Grimaldi	12 CSD		

Running No		date	maker	Rebodyings seats type		date	maker
11	(100)	1962	Vidler	12	CSD		
12	(34)	1966	RH & D/Sullivan	12	CSD		
13	(33)	1957	RH & D/Hooper	8	CSD	Reb	Everest 1962, Sullivan 1967
14	(17)	1961	RH & D/Everest	12	CSD		
15	(22)	1965	RH & D/Grimaldi	12	CSD		
16	(16)	1962	RH & D/Everest	12/	CSD		
17	(26)	1956	RH & D/Hooper	8	CHD		
18	(A2)	1963	Vidler	12	CSD		
19	(A4)	1965	RH & D/Grimaldi	12	CSD		
20	(1)	1964	Vidler	12	CSD		
21	(4)	1965	RH & D/Sullivan	12	CSD		
22	(7)	1963	Vidler	12	CSD		
23	(37)	1947	Kent & Sussex Woodcraft (Obs)	10	CHD	1967	RH & D/Sullivan 12 CSD
24	(25)	1956	RH & D/Hooper	8	CHD		
25	(30)	1962	RH & D/Everest	12	CSD	1966	RH & D/Sullivan 12 CSD
26	(38)	1947	as 23	10	CHD	1956	RH & D/Hooper 8 CHD
27	(36)	1956	RH & D/Hooper	8	CHD		
28	(A6)	1964	Vidler	12	CSD		
29	(18)	1956	RH & D/Hooper	8	CHD	Scr	30/4/73
30	(23)	1962	RH & D/Everest	12	CSD	Scr	16/1/73
31	(9)	1966	RH & D/Sullivan	12	CSD		
32	(19)	1961	RH & D/Everest	12	CSD		
33	(25)	1956	RH & D/Hooper	8	CHD	1971	RH & D/Allchin 12 CSD

(ii) *Standard 20-seat saloons*

51	1973	RH & D/Allchin	20 CSD
52	1973	Charlier, Hythe	20 CSD
53	1973	RH & D/Allchin	20 CSD
54	1973	RH & D/Allchin	20 CSD
55	1973	Charlier	20 CSD

(iii) *Clayton Wagon Co Pullmans*

110	1936	Rebuilt with	12 CHD	
111	1936	lowered roofs by RH & D	12 CHD	Withdrawn 5/72
112	1936		12 CHD	
113	1936	,,	12 CHD	Withdrawn 5/72
114	1936	,,	12 CHD	Withdrawn 5/72
115	1936	,,	12 CHD	
116	1936	,,	12 CHD	
117	1936	,,	12 CHD	

Running No	date	maker	Rebodyings seats type		date	maker

iv) Ex Hopper wagon coaches

Running No	date	maker	seats	type	date	maker
All:	1947	Kent & Sussex Woodcraft	18 or 20	CHD	As Pullman coaches, the first bodies on these frames. Subsequently as below:	
·00	1955	RH & D/Hooper	20	SO	1972	RH & D/Allchin 20 SO
·01	1955	RH & D/Hooper	20	SO	Scrapped 1972	
·02	1955	RH & D/Hooper	20	SO		
·03	1955	RH & D/Hooper	20	SO	1972	RH & D/Allchin 20 SO
·04	1955	RH & D/Hooper	20	SO	1972	RH & D/Allchin 20 SO

v) Open coaches

Running No	date	maker	seats	type	date	maker
·00	1946/7	RH & D	16	O		
·01	1946/7	RH & D	16	O		
·02	1946/7	RH & D	16	O	1971	RH & D/Allchin 16 O
·03	1946/7	RH & D	16	O		
·04	1946/7	RH & D	16	O		
·05	1946/7	RH & D	16	O	Scrapped 6/72	
·06	1946/7	RH & D	16	O	1971	RH & D/Allchin 16 O
·07	1946/7	RH & D	16	O		
·08	1946/7	RH & D	16	O	Scrapped 10/72	
·09	1896	A. P. Heywood	16	O	Never rebodied but much repaired	
·10	1946/7	RH & D	16	O		
·11	1946/7	RH & D	16	O	1972	RH & D/Allchin 16 O
·12	1946/7	RH & D	16	O		
·13	1946/7	RH & D	16	O		
·15	1946/7	RH & D	16	O	Scrapped 6/72	
·16	1946/7	RH & D	16	O	Scrapped 10/72	

vi) Queen Annes

Running No	date	maker	seats	type	date	maker
·00	1953/4	RH & D/Hooper	10	SO	Scrapped 1/73	
·01	1953/4	RH & D/Hooper	12	SO		
·02	1953/4	RH & D/Hooper	12	SO		
·03	1953/4	RH & D/Hooper	10	SO		
·04	1953/4	RH & D/Hooper	10	SO		
·05	1953/4	RH & D/Hooper	10	SO	Scrapped 3/73	
·06	1953/4	RH & D/Hooper	10	SO	Scrapped 10/72	
·98	1896	A. P. Heywood	10	SO	Withdrawn 1973	
·99	1904?	A. P. Heywood	16	SO		

Running No	date	maker	Rebodyings seats type	date	maker

(vii) *Gower-framed coaches* (first column is new condition)

Running No	date	maker	seats type	date	maker
800	1962	Vidler	16 CSD		
801	1962	Vidler	16 CSD		
802	1962	Vidler	16 CSD	Wdn 1973	
803	1962	Vidler	16 CSD		
804	1962	Vidler	16 CSD		
805	1962	Vidler	16 CSD	1972	RH & D/Allchin 16 CSD
806	1968	RH & D/Sullivan	16 CSD		
807	1968	RH & D/Sullivan	16 CSD		

NOTES: C= Closed; O= Open (roofed); SO= Semi-open.
HD= hinged doors; SD= Sliding doors.

It must be noted that over the next few years there will be much alteration to coaching stock, although no completely new frames are envisaged.

FREIGHT STOCK

As with the early passenger stock there are vaguenesses and uncertainties about the total number of wagons used by the railway during its early years. Building or modifying a 15in gauge wagon is a comparatively simple affair if wheels, axles and axleboxes are available so it is quite possible that wagons were added and scrapped from time to time without any record. The types on the other hand are clearly known and the tally would appear to be as follows:

Four-wheeled open wagons of Greenly design

Henry Greenly designed for the railway in 1926 a straightforward four-wheeled steel wagon underframe which was intended for a variety of uses: it was fitted as standard with a casting in the centre having a socket for a bolster pin if required and the drawbar-strain was taken by twin truss rods running from end to end. On this basic frame with some modifications, the following appear to have been built.

(i) Six one-cubic-yard capacity open wagons supplied by F. Theakston Ltd, in 1926. These had wooden planked bodies with side doors having distinctive 'c' shaped strapping. They were piped for running in passenger trains and were painted grey initially with 'RHDR' in white; this was later replaced on several by 'FISH ONLY' in white.

These wagons appear to have survived the war and three frames were still extant in 1973, two in the weedkilling train and one, numbered 207, in departmental use. The metal body parts of the three others were used in constructing three wagons for luggage Nos 205/6/? on well frames.

(ii) An undetermined number of wagons, probably 30, built up by Jackson, Rigby Ltd at New Romney during 1926-7; the patterns for many of the parts were extant at New Romney until recently. These were described as 'ballast wagons' and were used as such during construction. They had flat wooden platform bodies on which could be dropped Heywood-pattern, bottomless box-tops. As flat trucks they could be used for various purposes and some were fitted with metal strips and sockets to take bolsters. The 'tops' were initially painted grey with black corner strapping and white lettering but rapidly became bleached. Ministry returns (not always reliable) show a decline in number of about six in 1929-30 and it is likely that various frames were taken out of stock and simply used as trolleys. It appears certain that most of the survivors were placed under tipping skips after the war and were cut up about 1951. A few remained as wagons into the 1960s and their 'tops' were still extant on the rubbish dump in 1973.

(iii) An undetermined number, probably about 35, supplied through Theakston's after the war as part of an order for '50 coach and wagon frames'. These were bare chassis, were fitted with wooden dumb buffers and were used mainly to carry tipping 'skips' (qv). Most of the surviving wagon chassis at New Romney are of this batch. Dimensions of the basic underframe: length over headstocks 6ft 5in, width 3ft 4in, height varies.

Four-wheeled tipping wagons
(i) In the early days, Theakston's provided four $\frac{3}{4}$ cubic yard capacity side-tipping wagons with metal frames and bodies, two in 1925 and two in 1926. These were conventional V-bodied skips, were used in construction work, and then disappeared during the early 1930s.

(ii) After the war, in 1946, the railway went into business with the associated Romney Marsh Ballast Co, as related in chapter five. Initially it seems that the ballast company contributed about 30 large

V-shaped skips of one cubic yard capacity which were mounted on four-wheeled chassis provided by the railway; these were mainly the Greenly designed ballast wagon frames but included a small number —perhaps five or six—of well frames from the former articulated sets. These frames ran singly so had presumably been re-wheeled. As traffic built up another 30 or so skips were purchased complete from a firm in Manchester. (The exact proportions are uncertain but the total of skips was 60.) This second batch were mounted on their own wheels and axles, having very crude roller-bearing axle-boxes; intended for short push-lines they were not suited for RH & D speeds and there were several derailments when the wheels became loose on the axles and suddenly changed their gauge! In consequence the running gear was removed and the buckets and frames were mounted on four-wheeled underframes ordered in 1946–7 via Theakston.

In 1951, when rail ballast traffic stopped, the skips were split up between the partners. The ballast company sold its share for scrap and the other 30, all on Greenly frames, were taken into railway stock; a few were used for departmental purposes but most are disused; 17 survived in 1973.

Bogie wagons

Six bogie wagons were originally proposed but only two were actually built, in 1928–9, by Jackson, Rigby at New Romney. They were conventional open wooden wagons on steel frames and having drop sides which could be fitted with strakes to increase their height. Originally conceived for fish or sheep traffic, neither of which materialised to any degree, they were put into service as luggage wagons and were, accordingly, piped for the vacuum brake. After the war they were rebogied, one having Gibbins bogies, the other Hudson ones, and were fitted with mesh 'roofs' so that they could act as over-flow passenger-accommodation. Hardboard roofs were fitted later. In the 1952–3 renumbering they received Nos 200–1 and in 1966 they were withdrawn from traffic because of corroded frames. No 200 was scrapped at Christmas 1971. No 201 is still in pw service in 1973, however. Dimensions are: length over headstocks 18ft, width 3ft 3in, height 2ft 11in.

Bogie hopper wagons

In 1929 six six-ton capacity bogie steel hopper wagons were

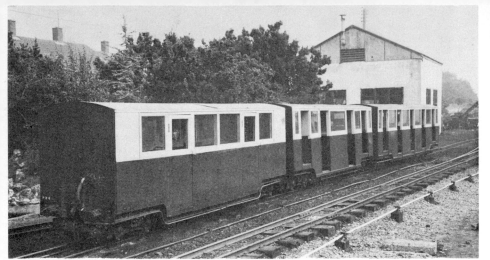

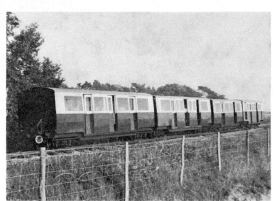

Page 143 (above) *L to R: Hooper 1956 8-seater; 'Queen Anne'; Hooper body on ex R & ER hopper wagon frame. 1973; (left) Sullivan-bodied 16-seater on Gower frame; Vidler-bodied ditto; Sullivan-bodied 8-seater; Everest-bodied 12-seater of 14/32 series; (below) Front row, L to R: Heywood open brake vehicle; Heywood closed bogie coach (as semi-open); Clayton Pullman as cut down; Heywood bogie open, with roof added. Back row, L to R: Clayton Pullman; van 500 as rebodied by Hooper; the Simplex tractor*

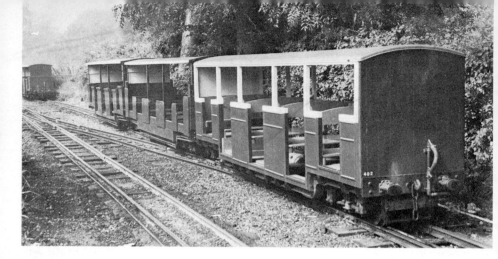

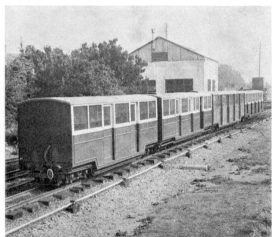

Page 144 (above) *Various opens (L to R): two types of post-war rebuild; 'standard' rebuild of 1972*; (left) *New Standard Stock (L to R): No 33; 16-seater on Gower frame; standard 20-seater; rebodied hopper wagon frame*; (below) *L to R: Ballast skip; Theakston (1926) wagon; Greenly four-wheeled underframe; Clifford Edwards well-frame; the Eaton Simplex*

purchased second-hand from the Ravenglass & Eskdale Railway through Theakston's. These were almost new vehicles, dating from 1928 and put out of service by the standard-gauging of the section of line over which they worked. At New Romney they were rebogied in 1930 with heavy duty Gibbins bogies and were then used for general service purposes, coupled in pairs. Unusually for the RH & D they retained their Heywood-pattern couplers but were not treated very well.

In 1936–7 they were overhauled for use in the projected ballast traffic and, since the bottom-discharge grids were not suitable for 'beach', holes were cut in their sides and fitted with top-hung doors, fabricated at New Romney. After ballast traffic ceased they became virtually derelict and were found as such by the Army in 1940. The frame of one was dismantled and used as part of a road block, two others were sent to Ashford Works (SR) and partially armour-plated for use in the armoured train (see chapter five). The remaining three remained in store until the war's end when all five were restored to use for the 1946 ballast traffic. After arrival of the final skips, in 1947, the bodies were stripped off and the frames used as the basis of new Pullman coaches (qv).

Four-wheeled well frames
It is difficult to know where to classify these frames. Apparently part of the 1946 Theakston order for '50 coach and wagon frames' there were about 12 to 15 of them and they were built by Clifford Edwards Ltd of Hove. They were similar to the original Greenly coach well frames but slightly shorter (9ft 6in) and were supplied unwheeled; 14in diameter wheels on axles, and roller bearing axle-boxes, were provided separately.

It appears that these were originally ordered as an experiment when ballast traffic was thought to be expanding, the idea being to lower the centre of gravity of the somewhat unwieldy skips. In practice all skips were in service when the frames were delivered in spring 1947 and they were never used as such. Instead they were kept stacked in the yard and were wheeled as required for various purposes: at least five appear never to have been wheeled at all and one bare frame was still acting as a carriage shed buffer stop in 1973. Of the others, four were made into 500 series brake vans—later 700 series coaches and then bare frames: one of these became a scooter frame in 1962. One frame became a platelayer's coach, then an open wagon; two were provided

I

with open wagon bodies about 1953. One was experimentally lengthened to act as a sleeper wagon but proved too rigid for the track. In 1973 nine frames survived: one never wheeled; one under the scooter; three under open wagons; and four as bare, wheeled underframes, one being the lengthened one.

Vans

The original guards vans, and the Heywood bogie brake van have been discussed already. There remain eight or nine vehicles plus one new acquisition.

(i) *1934-pattern vans*: Two matching luggage vans were supplied with the 54 Hythe saloon coaches in 1934–5, one being very quickly fitted with a Kohler generating set for providing electric light; it was marshalled in the Blue Train rake in 1938 and 1939. After the war, one van was fairly quickly rebuilt as an open coach (403). The other, subsequently numbered 500, has undergone various rebuildings and is at present a 'match' for the 1956-vintage stock. It is painted green and cream and dimensions are as for that stock.

(ii) *Heywood bogie luggage van*: This was a typical Heywood vehicle with a full-length wooden body on woodframes, and came from Eaton Hall in 1947. At New Romney it was cut down, small windows being inserted just below the roof line, and was used as a luggage vehicle in Pullman umber and cream. Latterly painted a drab green, it was condemned as unsafe to run in 1966 and was unfortunately broken up. Dimensions (original) were: length over headstocks 19ft 6in, width 3ft 6in, height 6ft.

(iii) *Heywood four-wheeled brake van*: Another relic of Eaton Hall, this small open vehicle had two back-to-back seats facing each end. It had a simple roof supported by pillars and breaking power was provided by a screwpillar handbrake between the seats. The vehicle was little used at Eaton Hall and even less at New Romney since it was too light to be really effective, although Howey used it for inspection purposes in his last years. At New Romney it lost its roof which was out of loading gauge but was otherwise in original condition when sold to a Mr Jacot in 1966. It ran on his private railway until 1972 when the stock of that line was bought by Mr W. A. McAlpine and returned to New Romney. During its absence it was painted brown and equipped with a vacuum brake but it has seen little use since its return. Dimensions as built were: width 3ft 6in, height to roof 6ft.

(iv) *Post-war brake vans*: As related on page 145 four half brake vans were built in 1952 on Clifford Edwards chassis to meet a ministry requirement that guards must have a brake under their control. The brakesman's part was little more than a crude hut over one compartment of a four-wheeled open coach and they lasted only until 1954. They were stored until conversion into open coaches.

MISCELLANEOUS VEHICLES

The railway has acquired a number of non-standard wagons at various times most of them never numbered into RH & D stock. Notable were an unknown number of four-wheeled Heywood-pattern open wagons from Eaton Hall, which came in 1947. Very few were ever put into service, most being broken up where they were dumped on arrival, in the up-side yard. Only one, of early pattern, survived complete in 1973 in departmental use but the chassis of one or two others were used for various purposes. There are also two partially rebuilt long-wheelbase flat wagons from the same source which are often referred to as 'carriage trucks'—though the load would have to have been a very small carriage!

At some time just prior to the war the railway also acquired the stock formerly used by WD personnel (see chapter four). This comprised a small scooter (qv), a small closed van and possibly a low-sided four-wheeled wagon; this latter, which only appeared on the railway after 1945 may, however, be built on the frame of one of the two scooters (qv). Its chassis is certainly almost identical and the 'body' was a very crude addition. The van disappeared early on and no details are available.

Lastly, in 1972, the stock of Mr Jacot's garden railway was bought by Mr W. A. McAlpine and brought to New Romney. It is not in RH & D stock but a number of small wagons are in casual use together with a vacuum-fitted four-wheeled brake van.

CHAPTER 10

Track and Fittings

GREENLY'S ACHIEVEMENTS

It is not often that one man gets a chance to design and build a complete public railway. In the Romney, Hythe and Dymchurch, Henry Greenly did get such a chance and it is a measure of his achievement that so much of his original work has survived the years; although somewhat overlaid by later alterations, the stamp of his work is so clear that it is possible for example even to recognise the Hythe station bus shelters immediately as of Greenly design.

Greenly's influence (other than on the locomotives!) is most clearly visible in his buildings, many of which survive. Although he never took formal qualifying examinations, he had been trained as an architect in 1898–9 at the London Polytechnic, and his buildings had a very characteristic appearance. It should be remembered that he had to work within the constraints of his period; just as the early 1900s were the corrugated iron age, so the 1920s and 30s were the era of suburban mock tudor—board and brick panelling with exposed wooden lath 'beams'. The style may not appeal nowadays but Greenly's work with it was at least honest. The wooden framing on his buildings was largely genuine, with brick or panel infilling, and where he did make use of lathwork for decoration—mainly on gable ends—he made no attempt to disguise its real nature. His original colour scheme of green and white is evidence of this.* He was also a pioneer of some renown in the structural use of concrete and his concrete bridges and retaining walls have proved almost indestructible, in some cases too much so when the railway has wished to make alterations. Again within the styling constraints of their period, they are clean, pleasant structures.

*Early references to blue and white cannot be confirmed.

148

In the writer's opinion, Greenly as an architect was at his best designing small structures. His larger buildings—Hythe station, New Romney station and offices, Red Tiles bungalow—are undistinguished if neat; they have little visual impact. Yet the minor buildings such as shelters, signal boxes and even the short-lived goods shed have a functional simplicity of line that appeals to the eye; the elegant curves supporting the shelter awnings are typical of his attention to detail. On a wider scale, a Greenly building can quickly be recognised by its 'trade-marks'. In particular he had a characteristic gable-end to his roofs with deep beams or barge boards making a shallow triangle that in larger buildings contained a series of vertical decorative laths; the whole was completed by a distinctive pointed wooden finial. Even the glassed ends of the original overall roofs showed this feature.

He also had a keen eye for the advantages of standardisation and the same design, in wood or brick, was repeated again and again around the railway. There were, in fact, only a few basic designs for minor buildings; an open shelter (page 107); a signal box (page 107); and a one- or two-roomed station building comprising shelter-cum-booking office. The design was built in weatherboarding or brick as conditions warranted and a typical contrast is that between the Botolph's Bridge shelter and those at New Romney.

In the layout of the line, too, Greenly's desire to conform with main line practice as a 'full-size miniature' railway was quite obvious. The LRO laid down rail standards (20lb/yd) and specified the need for home and distant signals but all the rest was Greenly. He actually used war surplus American and Belgian rail of about 24lb/yd acquired from a continental source and the route was laid out according to the civil engineering 'book', to give, for example, straight runs onto and off bridges. The stations were designed in imitation of main line practice, Greenly obviously envisaging that arriving trains would release their locomotives to shed while the stock was pulled out for servicing and then shunted back into a separate departure platform which would not need a release crossover at the buffer end. The original plan clearly did not suggest many trains and may have dated from the initial idea of a single track line. Turntable access was scrupulously achieved via a siding and not direct off the main line, and a proper independent bay loop was provided at the principal intermediate station so that short workings could be dealt with without interfering with main line traffic. Indeed, outside the termini, there were no facing points at all off the original main line.

The same concept was evident in Greenly's signalling arrangements of which practically nothing survives but the point-interlocking and the lever frames. The LRO may have required only home and distant signals but a main line railway clearly needed more. It was, indeed, very fully signalled, even including proper siding signals for goods yard and locomotive yard at New Romney, while all signals were interlocked with the appropriate points. In practice there was far too much signalling; even Dungeness, where visibility was limitless and trains could only go one way in any case, had its full complement to safeguard a very little used stock siding. The result was that at all but the main stations it fell into disuse and its provision was undoubtedly an error of judgement.

Inevitably, in undertaking such a mammoth task, Henry Greenly also made other errors, the biggest one being in the provision of small radius (125ft) points which proved difficult to negotiate. It may well be that he envisaged a small shunting locomotive such as *The Bug* working the sidings but again this was a misjudgement. The result was some very tortuous operating procedures. Indeed, so far as track was concerned, the system came under stress early on with the Dungeness extension and the amended traffic flows. The original concept did not survive Greenly's departure, Howey losing no time in drastically modifying the original elements. Buildings too underwent modification and much of Greenly's carefully planned signalling and point work was altered; it is not easy now to spot the care with which he arranged for the shortest possible 'pulls' and for the coupling of points into crossovers.

The subject, however, is interesting enough for this chapter to be devoted to a detailed examination of the main alterations over the years. It does not attempt to describe the atmosphere of the route today, which will be found in chapter seven but takes the major features one by one. The exact layouts of early days have proved phenomenally difficult to reconstruct with certainty. The following descriptions are the results of much research and discussion but even so I would not guarantee their infallibility; the 'Romney' had a habit of making ephemeral changes to suit the whims of its owner.

Hythe

As originally planned, Hythe terminus was laid out to provide the full main line facilities of which Greenly was so fond. The layout comprised a main arrival platform (No 2) with engine release road, a main departure platform (No 3) with no release facilities and a further platform road (No 4) with a locomotive release spur giving direct turntable access. From photographic evidence it seems that the northernmost platform road (No 1) was originally envisaged as an arrival platform since a two-armed bracket home signal was set up to control entry to platforms one and two. It also had a shunt arm controlling access to the 'down'-side of the station. If this is so, it was very soon changed since the platform road had no locomotive release and was awkward of access. The station boasted an overall roof, with a small booking office at the 'concourse' end and the platforms were originally gravelled and edged with stone. A 16-lever signal box was provided but no locomotive facilities other than the 30ft shallow-well turntable and an ordinary domestic water standpipe at the end of platform three. Hythe water was not considered suitable for the boilers and was used only in emergencies.

This layout has caused a great deal of discussion over the years, mainly in connection with the legend of the Sandling Branch. The author must here state his firm opinion that Greenly never made any provision for a Sandling extension in laying out Hythe. No powers were ever sought and well before the track got anywhere near Hythe the Sandling idea had been dropped as impracticable. The lie of the land is such that in any case a branch would have had to leave towards New Romney either from the up main line—which would have involved a long skewed crossing of the canal—or via the down line which would have needed a flyover. Frequent suggestions that the hypothetical branch might have left either end of No 1 road fail to take into account that if it ran out towards New Romney the canal crossing would have been difficult and incoming trains would have been in some danger of overshooting; an extension via Scanlon's Bridge would have been physically almost impossible.

In any case the Hythe layout soon proved inadequate to cope with traffic that required a four-train service, especially as the 125ft scissors crossover proved too sharp for the locomotives to negotiate easily. After the 1927 season it was replaced by a facing crossover of 150ft

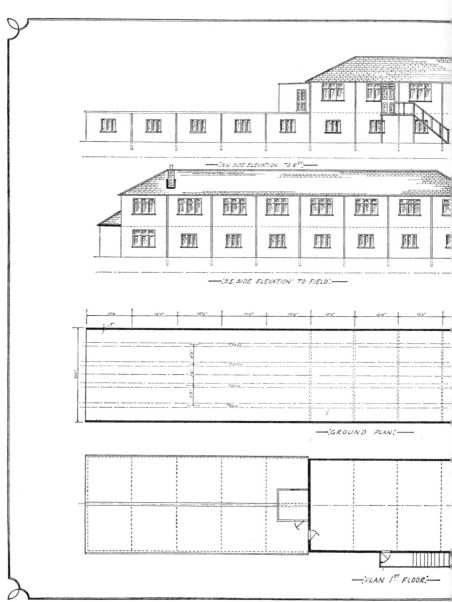

—NW. SIDE ELEVATION TO RLY.—

—SE. SIDE ELEVATION TO FIELD:—

—GROUND PLAN:—

—PLAN 1ST FLOOR:—

Original design for the 192

FRONT ELEVATION

—:PART LONGITUDINAL SECTION:—

—:CROSS SECTION AT 'A':—

OFFICE

OFFICE

—:CROSS SECTION AT 'B':—

MESS ROOM &
KITCHEN

OFFICE

LADIES

GENTS

GENTS

LADIES

—:PROPOSED CARRIAGE SHED: CLUB ROOM:—
—:AND OFFICES:—

—:R.H. & D. R^{wy} NEW ROMNEY, KENT:—

SCALE ⅛ = 1^{ft}   TRACED: A.L.S.R. 1919.20

shed and social club

radius in the same position and an engine release link was put in from No 3 platform road to allow arrivals and departures from there also. The home bracket signal was altered to control entry into platforms two and three, the small 'doll' mounted lower on the post being used as a shunt indicator for No 1 road; it was probably not interlocked with the points. No 1 road was then considered mainly as a stock siding and in spring 1928 was extended into the station forecourt specifically for fish traffic. A car park was laid in asphalt on the station forecourt and at about the same time the platform surfaces were concreted. During 1928 or early 1929 an additional crossover was laid in to give Nos 1 and 2 roads direct access to the down main line.

The layout remained unaltered until 1929. The major change was erection of a two-road shed of Greenly type for use as a paint shop in anticipation of alterations at New Romney. Meanwhile it was leased to the War Department (see page 51) and it was allowed to store its scooter there even after the shed was put into use. At the same time a connection was put in from the down main line to the turntable. Other alterations included the removal of the second turntable road between 1930 and 1932. It was replaced by a siding parallel to the road serving number four platform although a short spur was put in from the turntable to hold wagons of coal for use by the shuttle locomotives; this was enclosed by a wire cage and disappeared soon after the war. In 1933 the station roof was extended.

The next major modifications took place in 1936-7 winter, when a high level ballast hopper was put in on the south side with a long inclined siding leading to it. The siding had direct access to the main line but no catch points were installed. At the same time the siding next to number four platform road was altered to include a low sleeper-built ramp about midway along its length, for coach oiling, and was extended into the forecourt in front of the ballast hoppers. This allowed wagons to be positioned where they could be filled with any overspill littering the forecourt. Late in 1937, too, the water tank from Greatstone was brought to Hythe and positioned at the end of platforms three and four; it was soon afterwards moved to its present position by the signal box.

Apart from minor depredations caused by the military, Hythe saw little change thereafter until 1951. The ballast siding, slightly modified, was used for a short period in 1946-8 and then lay derelict until it was dismantled in 1951. An engine release road was at that time put in from number four platform to the turntable and the layout assumed its current (1973) form; the turntable itself was replaced by a deep 40ft one intended to take a projected 4–8–4 that was never built. The semaphore signals have been replaced by colour lights and in 1970 a former BR coach was set up in the forecourt as a railway shop. At the time of writing, plans are in hand to alter the physical appearance of the station considerably. The scheme allows for a new covered concourse with shopping and light buffet facilities and a new car park is envisaged at the departure end on some allotments. It is likely that access to this will involve taking No 4 platform out of service and removing the tracks alongside it.

One aspect of Hythe has not been mentioned although it may well puzzle visitors. The Light Railway Restaurant alongside No 1 platform road was contemporaneous with the railway and shows evidence of Greenly design features. It was originally the Light Railway Restaurant and Hotel and so far as is known was never owned by the railway, being the property of a Mr Farmer. It was initially a single storey building, the second floor being added before 1930. The two bus shelters fronting the road were also designed by Greenly and were erected by the railway to encourage those using bus connections.

HYTHE TO DYMCHURCH

At the exit to Hythe station, Greenly's original alignment took the track in a wide sweep as close as possible to the WD boundary along the Royal Military Canal. Howey considered that this gave a blind approach and in 1929–30 it was relaid further away to give a more open run; in this case the realignment involved more curves including a big reverse curve between Hythe Engineering Works and Prince of Wales Bridge. Here the line crosses under a road by a typical Greenly concrete bridge with separate tunnels for up and down trains. There was a cinder platformed halt here during 1927 and 1928 only.

The next constructional point of interest was $\frac{3}{4}$ mile on, at Palmarsh. When the line was being built much of the ballast was won from a bank near the present housing estate. This was close to the county council's West Hythe ballast facilities and it was envisaged that a fair traffic might develop. Greenly therefore planned and erected an eight-lever signal box of his normal design and a long curving siding was laid in on the seaward side. The only junction actually put in was a trailing connection to the down line, and this may have been removed after the line was opened. Palmarsh box was never more than a shell, being used by platelayers until 1947–8 when it was broken up. The disconnected siding was lifted in 1937.

Botolph's Bridge Halt

This was opened in 1927, consisting of a wooden shelter on the north side and cinder platforms. A cattle grid was provided soon after the opening but the level crossing was ungated. The halt was little used, soon became derelict and was officially closed in 1939. The hut had been burned down some two years earlier.

Burmarsh Road (Originally Burmarsh for East Dymchurch)

Planned as a full station, Burmarsh Road was typical of Greenly's practice. It had two gravelled platforms, concreted in 1928, with a two-roomed brick and wood building on the down-side. This acted as ticket office and waiting room containing a two-lever ground frame. Starting signals were provided on each platform but never connected to the frame. (These were presumably classed as combined homes and starters to comply with ministry requirements!) It was very soon downgraded to halt status and became unstaffed. The signals were removed and the building left to become derelict. The remains were pulled down in 1948 and the halt closed at the end of that season; except for a short period in 1950 it has not been used since. The land enclosed would indicate that a small goods yard was planned but there is no evidence this was ever installed; indications of a siding almost certainly date from the World War II years.

Dymchurch (Originally Dymchurch (Marshlands))

This was planned as the main intermediate station on the original railway and has always been a block section post. Again the concept was of a main line station and it was laid out to allow for through traffic with separate terminal facilities for short workings. Layout was as shown on page 195. The station had an overall roof and from 1928 to about 1933 a café—officially described as 'tea-rooms'—was sited on the up-side. It was reached from the up platform via a pair of french doors and was converted to a staff bungalow about 1934. The other station buildings were on the seaward side of the terminal bay but, for the 1927 season only, a temporary booking office was erected on the down main platform since the main approach was unfinished. The buildings were completed by a 12-lever signal box and a feature typical of Greenly's economic use of space—toilets concealed in the concrete piers of the station footbridge. The latter cannot have been conducive to quiet meditation on a busy day.

The provision of a footbridge may seem pretentious but it must be remembered that the running of expresses was envisaged. The actual layout was clearly intended to allow for short workings from the Romney direction but to avoid the use of facing points all trains arrived on the up main and then had to back over onto the down main before pulling into the bay. Home and starter signals were provided.

During 1927 it became obvious that short workings would originate mainly from Hythe. An additional crossover was put in early on at the Hythe end of the station and a refuge siding, with catch point, was installed on the up-side opposite the signal box. During winter 1927–8 the locomotive release line was removed from the bay sidings; the turntable apparently remained until the end of the 1929–30 season and it appears that a release spur was put in to the down main line. The table was little used, it being easier to run back to Hythe tender first, so it was removed during winter 1929–30 and re-used at New Romney.

The layout remained unaltered for many years, although signalling was slightly modified; the only change was the addition, in 1937–8, of a separate 10¼in layout near the old turntable site. During the war Dymchurch was headquarters for the Army units operating the line and various modifications took place. In particular concrete blast walls were cast inside the existing walls of the overall roof with the odd result that this now has windows on the outside but no sign of them within. A long Nissen hut was erected on the up-siding, the interlocking arrangements for signals and pointwork were dismantled and the signalling became derelict.

On page 195 a diagram shows the layout at it was soon after the war. In 1934 a kiosk had been built by the station building to replace the tearooms and this was reopened for sale of refreshments; a buffet shack was added in 1948. Signalling was restored and the Nissen hut removed before the 1947 season while the portion of footbridge over the 'bay', damaged in the war, was sealed off.

With the decision, in 1949, to run all short workings through to New Romney, Dymchurch declined sharply in importance. In 1962 the Hythe-end crossover was removed and the other one converted to local operation; it is normally kept locked. The footbridge was shortened to span only the main lines and the following year the signal box was pulled down. The essential signals were replaced by colour light ones operated from the station building. Since then a long shelter has been erected on the up platform, the catch point has been removed from the up-siding and the bay line has been shortened to a mere spur.

DYMCHURCH–NEW ROMNEY

Golden Sands Halt

This is a private halt serving Golden Sands Holiday Camp and was opened about 1948. It consists of a concreted alcove in the camp wall on the down side of the RH & DR.

St Mary's Bay

One of the original stations, it was intended to serve the big holiday camps in the area—particularly the Duke of York's camp at Jesson. It was originally known as 'Holiday Camp (for Jesson and St Mary's in the Marsh)' and up to the war was usually referred to as 'Jesson'. It consisted of two rail-level platforms with shelters and the regulation pair of signals; the up signal vanished early-on, the down one, presumably protecting the level crossing, lasted until the war. A longer shelter was erected on the up-side in 1950 using parts of an old carriage shed and another followed in 1962. It is still an established station and can be operated as a block post when required.

The only historical interest at St Mary's Bay is the frequent reference to a direct siding to the Duke of York's camp. There is no firm evidence at all that any such siding was ever built; it was certainly normal in early years for holiday camp specials to run forward empty to Dymchurch for remarshalling.

Between St Mary's Bay and New Romney there are two places of interest.

(i) The original bridge over New Sewer, a 56ft span girder bridge to the design of Henry Greenly and his son Kenneth. It was replaced in 1968 by the present structure. The approach tracks were laid out by Greenly in accordance with his principles to give a straight run on and off the bridge. This involved a long S curve that Captain

Howey considered unnecessary and the tracks were realigned to their
present position in 1929–30.

(ii) The Warren, where the railway burrowed under the main road by
a twin-tunnel concrete bridge; this has been somewhat modified in
1972–3 by roadworks. There was an ephemeral halt on the Hythe side
of the bridge during the 1927 season only. There are also physical
signs of a former siding from the down-side to a small ballast pit.

THE HUB OF THE LINE

New Romney
New Romney station is undoubtedly the most frustrating part of
the RH & DR for any historian to chronicle; the rapid, frequent and
drastic changes to buildings and layout were possible only on the 15in
gauge. They owe much to the early change of role, from terminus to
through station and something also to Howey's relationships with
Henry Greenly; in the space available here they can be summarised
only briefly.

(i) 1926–7: New Romney was originally laid out as a main line
terminus as shown on page 196; it grew to completion over a period
of some six or eight months so photographs of the period are mis-
leading. Simple but neat buildings which included offices, booking
facilities and toilets, fronted Littlestone Road and gave access to an
open circulating area by the rail-level platforms. There were four
platform roads—an arrival road with locomotive release and two
departure roads that had no release facilities but could be used also
for parking spare rakes of stock. A compact scissors crossover gave
quick access to the locomotive yard on the arrival side where facilities
included a 30ft turntable, a three-road locomotive shed, and a machine
shop without direct rail access. In accordance with Greenly practice,
handy spurs were provided off the turntable for storage of coal
wagons, etc. The departure (up)-side contained the goods trans-
shipment facilities at road level, a two road paintshop reached by
trailing points off the goods yard spur, and a four-road carriage shed.
The latter was a big Army-surplus wooden building initially reached
by a fan traverser linked to a trailing connection from the main line.
Like Greenly's contemporary traverser for Murthwaite Crushing
Plant on the Ravenglass & Eskdale, this was not a success and it was
replaced before the opening by a collection of small radius points.

All other buildings were characteristic Greenly wooden structures on high concrete bases, and the whole layout was controlled by a typical Greenly signal box with a 17-lever frame, sited centrally on the down-side of the station.

Even this basically simple layout was modified during construction; apart from the traverser incident, the paint shop originally had three tracks but with only one connected; this changed to two tracks reached from separate turnouts on the goods yard spur. There is a probably apochryphal story that, during the official Ministry inspection, Howey noticed suddenly that the spur, which climbed steeply, had no catch point; it was, so the story goes, rapidly installed while the inspector was entertained in a nearby bar! Since the same story has been told with specific reference to the later inspection of the Dungeness line also—and the venue has been placed at both New Romney and Dungeness—its authenticity is slightly doubtful. Yet true or not, the catch point for the spur in 1928 consisted of a complete full-size turnout pointing straight at the angle of the paint shop wall; had any loaded vehicle used it when running away the wooden building would have been in some jeopardy and the point was short-lived.

The goods yard layout is open to some conjecture but appears to have been finalised at that shown on page 196. The goods shed certainly had a track on the loading bank between it and the standard gauge; and since the remains of retaining walls in Greenly's characteristic large-aggregate concrete still exist, it is likely to have ended as a low-level rail trans-shipment siding. The big door was purely for use by road transport and the smaller, low level door at each end would indicate that a 15in gauge line went right through. There was certainly a high-level loading bank opposite the carriage shed, and the arrangement of sidings was clearly designed to minimise the possibilities of breakaways fouling the main line.

Signalling was comprehensive, the most impressive feature being the three-arm gantry bearing inner home signals. All signals appear initially to have had their numbers—or in one case their function ('loco') marked on the reverse in black. A fixed distant was sited some way out round the approach curve because buildings interfered with visibility of arriving trains. According to the inspector's reports this should have been yellow but it is doubtful if it ever was. The other signals were normal red and white.

(ii) 1928–9: The first drastic modification took place during winter

1927-8 when the Dungeness extension transformed New Romney into a through station with terminal bays. The layout is that shown on page 197. Alterations involved: removal of scissors crossover and replacement by a single crossover of 200ft radius; relocation of the main line with consequent removal of one terminal road which was replaced by a platform at a lower level with the original shelter mounted on it; rearrangement of the up-side works. The new crossover left no room for access to carriage shed No 1 so Greenly arranged for access through the paint shop and then via a traverser or a set of small radius points. The exact details are unclear but it appears the shed was used mainly for winter storage; additional cover was provided by a new severely functional shed with four roads on the down-side of the station. Note that entry to the original shed was always from the south; layouts showing a connection at the Hythe end are inaccurate and probably due to confusion with the later erecting shop.

In addition the building marked CW in the diagram on page 196 was also brought round to the position shown, apparently with the intention of making it into a carriage workshop and connecting it to the carriage sidings. A suggested layout by Greenly shows this but in practice the building was left outside the boundary for several years and used by Captain Howey for other purposes. The goods shed was not altered but the whole yard was shored up with a retaining wall. A set of trailing points was installed in the standard gauge siding with the intention of providing a short spur for wagon storage but it appears this was never laid.

Last but not least, a new up platform was provided in the form of a complete small station beyond the Littlestone Road tunnels. Considerable problems were encountered in finding a route past the SR station, the main road having to be raised some four feet although this still left the narrow gauge in a deepish cutting. The up platform was fitted into one side of this and had a footbridge giving access to the SR and to the lane leading up to the main road, while a larger overbridge was built to pass sheep from the lane to a cattle dock in the standard gauge station. As originally built, the station had its own booking office and bore the legend 'Littlestone on Sea and Southern Railway. New Romney Station Opposite'. It lasted only for the 1928 and 1929 seasons, being awkward to run and inconvenient to staff. It has, however, helped to cause a good deal of confusion for its name— a sop to the Southern Railway's urge of the period to end at seaside

K

resorts—was perpetuated on most RH & D publicity until the war. The main RH & D station certainly bore similar nameboards until the mid-1930s though by 1936 rather warped 'New Romney' signs were again in evidence. For convenience it is referred to as New Romney hereafter.

(iii) 1929–34: The new layout was inconvenient and in winter 1929–30 another drastic upheaval took place; it was preceded by modification of the engine shed layout after an incident when Northern Chief derailed on the turntable, locking all locomotives in the shed. First one and then two roads were hastily diverted round the table.

The main upheaval was caused by straightening the main lines to remove the ferocious curves and to ease the gradient. The result is shown on page 198. Briefly the whole up-side works was swept away, the carriage shed disappearing while the paint shop, suitably modified, was re-erected over the arrival roads of the former terminal station as a carriage shed. The goods spur was relocated, a short up platform being tucked in between it and a new overall roof similar to that at Dymchurch. A foot crossing linked the platforms and a spring-loaded crossover opposite the disused up station linked the running lines. Most short workings then arrived at and departed from what is now platform three.

On the up-side, an ornamental rock garden hid the worst scars and a utilitarian steel and concrete erecting shop was put up roughly on the site of the old paint shop. Access was from the Hythe end and the former Dymchurch turntable was incorporated in it. An employees' social club was built on the flat roof of the 'new' carriage shed (it now houses Modelland) and offices were constructed at its southern end. Lastly, the signalling was completely recast. A 24-lever frame had replaced the original 17-lever one when the Dungeness line was built but this was now underused. The gantry was replaced by a tall lattice-post signal and a very tall signal using SR arms was installed by the tunnels to give adequate sight lines for drivers of both up and down trains. The old terminal station retained its signals but they were disused and the platforms were used only for stock storage. The former main line approach, now a trailing spur off the down main line, acted as a headshunt giving access only to the running shed and carriage sidings.

(iv) 1935–on: During winter 1934–5 it appears that the goods shed and trans-shipment yard were demolished, replaced by a low-level siding. Part of the retaining walls had gone, access to the erecting shop now being via a pair of points; the turntable had been moved across to the down-side to replace the original locomotive shed turntable, in bad repair after nearly ten years of continual use. From 1935 onwards, the alterations were comparatively minor. Specifically, the 'dormitory' was brought within the boundary fence and rail-connected via trailing spur from the carriage sidings (1936–7). The running shed turntable was replaced on a different site during winter 1936–7 by the former Pilton Works turntable of the Lynton & Barnstaple Railway and the approach lines were altered at the same time. The ex-Dymchurch turntable appears likely to have gone to Hythe to replace the original there. New SR-type signals replaced several of the former arms.

Except that solid blast walls were built to enclose the overall roof on the down-side in 1940, the station remained in this state until after the war. More recent alterations have not significantly altered the appearance and only three need detailed mention. A footbridge was built in 1948 north of the overall roof; the original main line was extended past the locomotive sheds in 1949 and once more connected to the down line. In 1965–6 the up platform was extended along the cutting, the footbridge being moved to its present position in 1966. From 1949 the existing semaphore signals have gradually been replaced by colour lights and by 1966 the only surviving semaphore was No 13 which has since vanished.

The other post-war alterations are:

1946: Line singled beyond old 'up' station, with spring-loaded points.
1949–50: Carriage shed over old terminal station pulled down.
1949–51: Ballast hopper and siding put in behind main carriage shed, scrapped 1951.
1958–9: New two-road paint shop built on down-side.
1961: Locomotive shed extended to 125ft.
1965–6: Long shelter provided on up platform.
1966–7: Up-side stock sidings relaid and proper awning built, replacing a former lean-to.
1966–8: Café built beside Modelland over the main carriage shed.
1967: (March) SR branch closed. SG siding lifted.
1971: Former machine shop internally reconstructed.

1973: Two-road carriage shop extended. One-road shop has rail access removed.

It should be noted that plans are being studied for another fairly drastic rebuilding at the time of writing.

NEW ROMNEY–DUNGENESS

When considering this section it must be remembered that since 1946 the line has been single, on the site of the old down road. After 1952 there were no turnouts between New Romney and Britannia Points. For two years only (1950–51) there was a siding, trailing from Hythe, which left the main line about a quarter mile south of New Romney and climbed steeply to enter the Ballast Works still visible on the down-side. The siding formation is still discernible in the undergrowth.

Greatstone on Sea (9·6m) (Originally Greatstone Dunes)
When the Dungeness extension was built, big developments were expected here and a proper station was laid out. (Diagram on page 201.) The eight-lever frame from Palmarsh signal box, was installed in a combined station building-cum-signal box, a footbridge was partly built—no steps being fitted—and a siding, presumably for goods, was put in on the up-side. Home and starter signals were provided and there was a water tank so it appears that some trains were expected to terminate here. A single crossover was provided but there were no run-round facilities.

In the event it was clear even by the opening date that the expected traffic would not materialise. The points were never connected up to the frame and the footbridge was not completed though the usual Greenly toilets in its piers were brought into use; it did act as a gantry for the up starting signal. The station was staffed during the high season but the water tank was removed to Hythe in 1937 and during the war the Army virtually wrecked the place; they installed a massive pillbox on the up platform incorporating bits of Greenly shelter as a camouflage.

After 1946, Greatstone became a single-line halt although it was manned during the high season until about 1965. It was then allowed to decay and the vandalised and derelict building, from which all fittings had long since gone, was demolished in 1971. The site is currently (1973) simply a cleared space and a nameboard.

Maddieson's Camp

Next point of note is the halt for Maddieson's Holiday Camp. Officially Maddieson's Littlestone Camp, this is actually about three-quarters of a mile past Greatstone station. It has always been a big summer customer but the only facilities provided up to 1973 were a cleared space and a nameboard by the camp entrance. Until 1937 this halt alternated summer and winter with Lade Halt in the time-tables. Plans are currently in hand (1974) for a passing loop and basic passenger facilities to be installed.

Lade Halt (11m)

This halt, provided for the opening, had a Greenly pattern shelter which disappeared during or soon after the war. The 'platform' is on the up-side and now has a small concrete shelter built in 1968.

Beween Maddieson's and Lade there was from 1929 to 1951 a siding curving off from the up line and crossing the shingle to ballast pits on the far side of the SR branch. It was originally laid for WD use but after the war was used for ballast traffic. It was lifted in 1951 and a rough road now occupies most of its course. The underbridge on the derelict SR branch is still visible, this having been put in when the SR modified their alignment in 1937.

From this point the railway originally ran across open shingle. There were few roads but development in the 1930s caused the railway to provide two overbridges before The Pilot Halt in 1938. Some 300 yards before the halt is reached there was, for a few months only, a turning triangle on the up-side; the road-bed is still (1973) visible.

The Pilot (12·6m)

This was from April to August 1928 the temporary terminus but was always intended as a small wayside station. It had cleared shingle 'platforms' and a two-roomed brick-and-wood Greenly building fronted by a strip of concrete that extended to the level crossing. The building was in use as a staff dwelling by 1934 and was also used as staff accommodation for several years after the war but was then allowed to fall derelict. The remains were demolished in 1967 and were replaced by a small concrete shelter in 1968.

It appears that for some years there was also a short siding at this point. Certainly provision was made for one on the original plans, a special variation in the deviation limits being included; newspaper references mention a 'fish siding' being built in spring 1928 and a company plan (page 44) dated 4 September 1928 shows a long siding, with junction facing to Hythe, leaving the halt and extending in front of the fishermen's shacks just above high water mark. If it existed it did not survive for long but its presence may well explain the 15in gauge track currently in use for some of the fishermen's trolley lines. On the other hand the material may have been reused in another siding at Dungeness (qv).

Dungeness (13·75m)
It is convenient to take the whole southern end of the railway as coming within this description. As originally laid out the southern terminus consisted of a huge balloon loop across the shingle, with station buildings almost in the shadow of the lighthouse. There were originally no intermediate track facilities though a halt existed ephemerally at the loop throat in 1928–9. In 1929 a stock siding was added within the loop and this still exists. The station buildings, ready even before track was laid, comprised a small booking office, a standard Greenly signal box controlling five signals and two points, a small shelter and, surprisingly, a separate toilet building. A water tank was provided, fed via a wind-pump, and the ensemble was completed by a large café with living accommodation above. The siding trap point was similar to that at Dymchurch in that it had no frog.

As at Greatstone the elaborate signalling facilities were not really needed and were disused by about 1930, the main gantry being transferred to New Romney by 1931. For some years in the 1930s a pair of points was inserted at the loop throat each winter, thus cutting off the up line for WD use, maintenance, etc. For a short period, between 1937 and the war, a long siding also left the loop via a facing junction to terminate by new weigh-houses and an SR extension at a point near the present Britannia Inn. The trackbed is still visible. It appears to have been put in for ballast or fish traffic but was little used.

The Dungeness end of the railway suffered severely during the war and in the late 1940s the station changed markedly. The shelter disappeared, the wind-pump was dismantled in 1951 and the water tank transferred to the roof of the gents' toilets in 1947. The signal box was converted to ladies' toilets, lasting as such until 1967. In 1961 a long roof was built over the rail-level platform which was concreted, and since then the original booking office has been replaced by a hut on the same site.

CHAPTER 11

Timetables and Train Working

The early timetables of the RH & DR were frankly experimental and reflected the promoter's ideas of running a main line railway. A frequent and regular service was provided between Hythe and New Romney during the 1927 season, the first departure from New Romney being as early as 6.30am. First train from Hythe was at 7.15 and there was virtually a shuttle service of trains until the last departure at 9.20pm from Hythe. Journey time was 30 minutes and the company expressed its intention of running trains up to 11pm when headlights had been fitted to the locomotives.

No details are available of the 1927 winter service which would in any case have been hampered by work on the Dungeness extension but the 1928 summer service (initially to Dungeness 'Pilot' and then to 'Lighthouse') was very comprehensive and elaborate. The full service was reprinted no less than three times under the headings 'Dungeness–Hythe'; 'New Romney–Hythe'; and 'Dungeness–Dymchurch'. Nineteen trains each way were provided on the Hythe section, the first train out of New Romney being at 7.25am (weekdays only), and 13 ran through to Dungeness with an extra late-evening train at 9.30pm on Saturdays only. The main oddity was that New Romney was so called in the timetables but in the footnotes was referred to as RH & D Railway Littlestone Station. The following years appear to have been very similar.

By the early 1930s, services had settled down somewhat and the summer 1932 timetable reproduced below (page 169) shows a number of points of interest. It will be seen that the early morning trains have disappeared, the first departure from New Romney now being 9.30am, although there is still a late evening working from Hythe. The basic service was 13 trains daily, five of which were extended to Dungeness. An interesting feature perpetuated in later years was provision for up to eight short conditional workings between Hythe and Dymchurch—the WP or 'weather permitting' shuttles that were run at peak periods. Since the locomotive for these was based at New Romney, the first and last shuttle working ran from and to that place. Another feature was the regular termination of some trains at

ROMNEY, HYTHE AND DYMCHURCH RAILWAY

Dungeness	...				12 0							415	5 0	6 0 7 30
The Pilot	...				12 5							420		6 5 7 35
Maddison	...	9 45	11 0	1145 1210	1245	145	245 315	425				610 740
Greatstone	...	9 50	11 5	1150 1215	1250	150	250 320	430				615 745
			wP									
Littlestone	...	9 30 10 0 1030 1115	12 0 1230	1 0	2 0	3 0 330	445	530	630 8 0
Jesson	...	9 38 10 8 1038 1123	12 8 1238	1 8	2 8	3 8 338	453	538	638 8 8
			wP		wP		wP		wP	wP	
Dymchurch	...	9 45 1015 1045 1130 1150 1215 1245 1 0 1 15 150 215 250 315 345 415 5 0 515 545 6 0 645 815
Burmarsh	...	9 50 1020 1050 1135 1155 1250 1250 1 5 1 20 155 220 255 320 350 420 5 5 520 550 6 5 650 820
Hythe	...	10 0 1030 11 0 1145 12 5 1230 1 0 115 1 30 2 5 230 3 5 330 4 0 430 515 530 6 0 615 7 0 830

		wP		wP		wP			r		wP	
Hythe	... ...	1030 11 0 1130 12 0 1230 1 0 130 2 0 230 245 315 340 4 0 430 5 0 535 6 0 630 7 0 745 9 0
Burmarsh	...	1040 1110 1140 1210 1240 110 140 210 240 255 325 350 410 440 510 545 610 640 710 755 910
Dymchurch	...	1045 1115 1145 1215 1245 115 145 215 245 3 0 330 355 415 445 515 550 615 645 715 8 0 915
Jesson	... ...	1052 1122	1222	122	222	3 7 337	422 452	622 652 722 8 7 922
Littlestone	...	11 0 1130	1230	130	230	315 345	430 5 0	630 7 0 730 815 930
Greatstone	...	11 6 1136	1236	136	236	321	5 6	636 7 6
Maddison	... ...	1111 1141	1241	141	241	326	511	641 711
The Pilot	...	1118				333	518	648
Dungeness	...	1130				345 4 0	530	7 0

wP—Dymchurch only, weather permitting.   x—Cheap Excursion to Dungeness.

Summer 1932 timetable

Maddieson's Camp. These trips provide a number of puzzling points. There was never, so far as is known, any pointwork at Maddieson's so the stock was presumably propelled in one direction. It would appear that partial wrong line working was in force in one direction, since on two occasions the Maddieson's–New Romney working passed a down Dungeness train at Greatstone. Greatstone crossover was probably used to cross the short working onto the up line there. Lastly a cheap evening excursion to Dungeness was advertised, another feature perpetuated in future years. Indeed the Dungeness service required that at one period two trains were standing at the terminus.

Up to 1940 the railway ran a regular winter service, the one operated for most of the time being similar to that shown on page 170. This is noteworthy mainly for the fact that Lade Halt regularly replaced Maddieson's Camp in winter as an advertised stop and for the fact that the timetable could be covered by one locomotive. This was usually the Rolls-Royce petrol tractor.

By 1935 the main summer timetable showed a few changes of interest. There were only three daily trains through to Dungeness—one in the morning and two in the afternoon, one of which was a cheap excursion. The late evening working to and from Hythe was

R. H. & D. Railway.   WINTER TIME TABLE

	Mon.—Fri.			Saturdays only.						
Dungeness	...	...	...	...	...	1 45	...		...	7 50
Pilot	...	...	...	...	...	1 50	...		...	7 55
Lade	...	...	...	...	...	1 57	...		...	8 02
Greatstone	...	...	...	...	...	2 00	...		...	8 05
Littlestone	930	2 00	5 15	930	1200	2 10	3 15	5 30	8 10
Jesson	938	2 08	5 23	938	1208	2 18	3 23	5 38	8 18
Dymchurch	945	2 15	5 30	945	1215	2 25	3 30	5 45	8 25
Burmarsh	950	2 20	5 35	950	1220	2 30	3 35	5 50	8 30
Hythe	1000	2 30	5 45	1000	1230	2 40	3 45	6 00	8 40

	Mon.—Fri.			Saturdays only.						
Hythe	1200	4 30	6 00	1030	1 00	2 45	4 30	7 00	9 00
Burmarsh	1210	4 40	6 10	1040	1 10	2 55	4 40	7 10	9 10
Dymchurch	1215	4 45	6 15	1045	1 15	3 00	4 45	7 15	9 15
Jesson	1222	4 52	6 22	1052	1 20	3 05	4 52	7 22	9 22
Littlestone	1230	5 00	6 30	1100	1 25	3 10	5 00	7 30	9 3
Greatstone	...	...	...	...	1 30	...	...	7 35	...
Lade	...	...	...	...	1 33	...	...	7 38	...
Pilot	...	...	...	...	1 40	...	...	7 45	...
Dungeness	...	...	...	...	1 45	...	...	7 50	...

The trains given on this time table are run right through the winter months. For Summer time table see Page 3.

A typical winter service timetable of the 1930s

reduced to a Saturdays Only 'when required' and the eight WP shuttles were now marked 'R' 'if required'. A timetable misprint gave the impression these workings were unbalanced, with only six in one direction and it misled passengers in another way also. The Maddieson's workings were discontinued according to the timetable leaflets but in practice they still ran and were advertised locally. At this time, moreover, it was not uncommon for some trains to be run in two parts, notably the 4.30pm excursion from Hythe and its return working. It must be remembered that the summer season was short then, from the beginning of July to the end of September, that trains were generally shorter than today and that the number of passengers per train was fewer. It is also worth noting that the fares remained unchanged for nearly fifteen years; the fare table below was typical while cheap excursions to Dungeness cost only 2/- (10p) return from Hythe and 1/- (5p) from Littlestone. Regular party fare reductions were also made although it is noticeable that the original 'sporting' offer of special trains for more than four people had been quietly dropped.

Fares to and from All Stations

	D'ness	Pilot	L'stone Camp	Greatstone	Li'lestone	H'll'd y Comp	Dymchurch	Burmarsh	Hythe
Dungeness	...	4d	6d	6d	8d	11d	1/-	1/2	1/6
		6d	**1/-**	**1/-**	**1/4**	**1/10**	**2/-**	**2/4**	**3/-**
The Pilot	4d	...	6d	6d	6d	9d	10d	1/-	1/4
	6d		**1/-**	**1/-**	**1/-**	**1/6**	**1/8**	**2/-**	**2/6**
Littlestone Holiday Camp	6d	6d	...	6d	6d	9d	11d	1/-	1/4
	1/-	**1/-**		**1/-**	**1/-**	**1/6**	**1/10**	**2/-**	**2/6**
Greatstone	6d	6d	6d	...	4½d	5d	8d	9d	1/-
	1/-	**1/-**	**1/-**		**6d**	**10d**	**1/4**	**1/6**	**2/-**
Littlestone	8d	6d	6d	4½d	...	4½d	5d	6d	10d
	1/4	**1/-**	**1/-**	**6d**		**6d**	**10d**	**1/-**	**1/8**
Holiday Camp	11d	9d	9d	5d	4½d	...	4½d	4½d	9d
	1/10	**1/6**	**1/6**	**10d**	**6d**		**6d**	**6d**	**1/6**
Dymchurch	1/-	10d	11d	8d	5d	4½d	...	4½d	8d
	2/-	**1/8**	**1/10**	**1/4**	**10d**	**6d**		**6d**	**1/3**
Burmarsh	1/2	1/-	1/-	9d	6d	4½d	4½d	...	7d
	2/4	**2/-**	**2/-**	**1/6**	**1/-**	**6d**	**6d**		**1/2**
Hythe	1/6	1/4	1/4	1/-	10d	9d	8d	7d	...
	3/-	**2/6**	**2/6**	**2/-**	**1/8**	**1/6**	**1/3**	**1/2**	

Heavy Type Figures denote Return Fares

The standard pre-war fare table

Neither this nor any other published timetables completely reflect the complexity of the railway's operations. Then as now it was common for regular 'special' trains to be run for the holiday camp proprietors a typical example being the Fridays-only morning train for arriving and departing children at Jesson Camp. The Southern Railway provided a special working from New Romney at 8.30am and the RH & D made a connection; customarily this was a massive double-headed affair that was propelled empty coaching stock (ECS) to Jesson and then run back on the correct line. A reverse working later brought incoming campers from New Romney but in that case the train ran on ECS to Dymchurch to water and run round.

The 1936 timetable (page 173) is of special interest in that it was the first to need six engines in service at one time. Although *Hercules* may have been outshopped during the season, there were normally only seven steam and one petrol engines to cover the normal timetable and all specials, which must have thrown quite a strain on the operating department.

The 1937 and 1938 timetables differed again, Lade first appearing as an advertised additional stop in 1937. In particular clearly defined periods covered the peak period (16 July–10 September or roughly the school holidays), and the early and late summer. At peak period no less than 18 regular trains left Hythe daily, 11 running through to Dungeness and one going only to Dymchurch. Crack train was the 2.45pm to Dungeness calling only at Dymchurch and New Romney (the Blue Train) and returning from Dungeness at 4.20pm; it took 50 minutes for the single trip as opposed to 60 minutes for normal trains. As usual there were seven advertised Hythe–Dymchurch shuttles 'when required' during the peak period only and no less than four late afternoon and evening cheap excursion trains to Dungeness ('visitors are allowed to inspect the lighthouse entirely at the discretion of the keeper-in-charge'). An innovation was provision of a cheap day return from Dungeness line stations, available only by the 11.25am ex-Dungeness in the peak and by the 10.50am at other times. The 1939 service was similar and a normal winter timetable was worked in 1939–40 until the area was evacuated.

Military trains did run to timetable during the war for troop transport and recreational purposes but few details are available. It appears that the 1942 timetable—or departure sheet—was typical, this advertising departures simultaneously from Hythe and Dungeness at 2.0, 3.0, 4.40, 5.40 and 9.30pm, the last train running on Sundays only. Journey time was one hour, fifteen minutes.

The daily winter service was not resumed after the war and in 1946 a fairly restricted service operated between Hythe and New Romney only, with a few trains extended to Maddieson's Camp. These and their successors in later years were definitely propelled back from Maddieson's over the single line and normally consisted only of two or three coaches. Full summer service was resumed in 1947 and the timetable was divided into early-and-late and peak periods, the latter being from 29 June to 6 September. Even in the

PUBLIC TIMETABLE FOR PEAK PERIOD 1936

Down — Hythe to Dungeness (column marked *R* near the right-hand end = "If Required")

Hythe	10.30 11.00 12.00 1.00 2.00 2.45 3.15 4.00 4.30 5.15 6.00 6.25 6.45 7.30 *9.00*
Burmarsh Road	10.40 11.10 12.10 1.10 2.10 2.55 3.25 4.10 4.40 5.25 6.10 6.35 6.55 7.40 *9.10*
Dymchurch	10.45 11.15 12.15 1.15 2.15 3.00 3.30 *4.15* 4.45 5.30 6.15 6.40 7.00 7.45 *9.15*
Jesson	10.50 11.20 12.20 1.20 2.20 3.05 3.35 4.50 5.35 6.20 6.45 7.05 7.50 *9.20*
Littlestone	9.30 10.30 11.00 11.30 *12.30* 1.30 2.30 3.00 3.15 3.45 4.45 5.00 5.45 6.15 6.30 6.55 7.15 8.00 *9.30*
Greatstone	9.35 10.35 11.05 11.35 1.35 2.35 3.05 3.50 4.50 5.00 6.20 6.35
Maddieson's	9.38 10.38 11.10 11.38 1.38 2.38 3.08 3.53 4.53 6.23 6.40
Pilot	9.45 10.45 11.20 11.45 1.45 2.45 3.15 4.00 5.00 6.50
Dungeness	9.50 10.50 11.30 11.50 1.50 2.50 3.20 3.35 4.05 5.00 5.20 7.00

Up — Dungeness to Hythe (column marked *R* near the left-hand end = "If Required")

Dungeness	9.50 10.50 12.00 12.45 1.50 3.20 4.10 4.30 5.05 6.15 7.30
Pilot	9.55 10.55 12.05 12.50 1.55 3.25 4.15 5.10 7.35
Maddieson's	10.02 11.02 12.15 12.57 2.02 3.32 4.22 5.17 7.45
Greatstone	10.05 11.05 12.20 1.00 2.05 3.35 4.25 5.20 7.50
Littlestone	9.30 10.10 10.35 11.10 12.30 1.10 2.10 3.10 3.30 *3.40* 4.00 4.30 4.50 5.25 6.00 6.35 8.00
Jesson	9.35 10.15 10.40 11.15 12.35 1.15 2.15 3.15 3.35 4.05 4.55 6.05 6.40 8.05
Dymchurch	9.45 10.25 10.50 11.25 12.45 1.25 2.25 3.25 3.45 4.15 4.40 5.05 6.15 6.50 8.15
Burmarsh Road	9.50 10.30 10.55 11.30 12.50 1.30 2.30 3.30 3.50 4.20 4.45 5.10 6.20 6.55 8.20
Hythe	10.00 10.40 11.05 11.40 1.00 1.40 2.40 3.40 4.00 4.30 4.55 5.20 6.30 7.05 8.30

R = If Required = 'R' shuttles leave Hythe (for Dymchurch) 11.30, 12.30, 2.30, 3.30, 5.00
'R' shuttles leave Dymchurch (for Hythe) 12.00, 1.00, 3.00, 4.00, 5.30

off-season a substantial service was provided, with nine regular trains between New Romney and Hythe, three being extended to Dungeness and one to Maddieson's with a further extension to Dungeness on Saturdays only. There was also a late evening departure from Hythe on Saturday at 8.30pm; this ran through to Dungeness for local passengers only and returned to New Romney ECS. The high season timetable gave twelve regular trains with five working through to Dungeness (six on Saturdays), and four returning. Short workings were as in the off season but the main item of note was the inauguration of a non-stop express The Bluecoaster Limited from Hythe to Dungeness in 45 minutes (dep: 2.30pm, return at 3.45). This was treated as a supplementary fare train with all seats bookable in advance and carried an observation car. From this time on the shuttles were not included in the timetables but were run as required.

The 1949 timetable shows a more settled pattern and is given in full (on page 175). It will be noticed that the main season has been extended but with some trains running at peak periods only; that the Bluecoaster no longer charges a supplementary fare; and that the halts have been dropped from the timetable although they were still open.

There was not a great deal of variation in the services during the 1950s and 1960s once a general pattern had been established except that shuttles, when worked, normally ran through to and from New Romney instead of terminating at Dymchurch. After the Captain died in 1963 there was a slow but steady consolidation of the service, times being adjusted to reduce both the number of locomotives in steam and their annual mileage where possible. By the late 1960s a different pattern had emerged, requiring only four locomotives in service at any one time; 1969 was the last year in which a named train (The Blue Train) was run and this was in reality simply a specified rake which worked a full diagram—including the, now Fridays only, morning train from Dungeness.

The early 1970s have seen further adjustments. Basically, up to 1972, these have included extension of the operating season, with a skeleton service from Easter onwards, and the assimilation into the timetable, from 1972-on, of the former shuttles. The 1973 timetable showed yet further adjustments with early, middle and peak periods and this is likely to be the pattern for future years. At peak it offers five journeys to and from Dungeness daily with an additional morning trip on Fridays for shoppers and a total of fifteen return journeys between Hythe and New Romney. One of these last does not run on

SUMMER TIME TABLE
From 19th May to 2nd October, 1949

UP

		a.m.	a.m.		a.m.	p.m.		p.m.	p.m.	p.m.,
Dungeness ...	dep.	—	—	—	—	12 00	—	—	—	2 00
Maddieson's Camp	dep.	—	10 10	—	—	12 10	—	—	—	2 10
Greatstone ...	dep.	—	10 15	—	—	12 15	—	—	—	2 15
New Romney { arr.		—	10 25	—	—	12 25	—	A	B	2 25
New Romney { dep.		9 30	10 30	—	11 30	12 30	—	1 45	2 00	2 30
St. Mary's Bay ...	dep.	9 38	10 38	—	11 38	12 38	—	1 53	2 08	2 38
Dymchurch ...	dep.	9 45	10 45	—	11 45	12 45	—	2 00	2 15	2 45
Hythe	arr.	10 05	11 05	—	12 05	1 05	—	2 20	2 35	3 05

UP

		B	A		A	A			B	A
		p.m.	p.m.		p.m.	p.m.	p.m.		p.m.	p.m.
Dungeness ...	dep.	3 00	3 30	—	4 00	4B15	5A00	—	5 50	6 00
Maddieson's Camp	dep.	—	—	—	Z	—	5A10	—	6 00	6 10
Greatstone ...	dep.	—	—	—		—	5A15	—	6 05	6 15
New Romney { arr.		3 20	3 50	—	The Bluecoaster Limited	4B35	5A25	—	6 15	6 25
New Romney { dep.		3 30	3 55	—		4 40	5 30	—	6 20	6 30
St. Mary's Bay ...	dep.	3 38	4 03	—		4 48	5 38	—	6 28	6 38
Dymchurch ...	dep.	3 45	4 10	—		4 55	5 45	—	6 35	6 45
Hythe	arr.	4 05	4 30	—	4 45	5 15	6 05	—	6 55	7 05

DOWN

						A	B	A	B	A
		a.m.	a.m.	p.m.	p.m.	p.m.	p.m.	p.m.	p.m.	p.m.
Hythe	dep.	10 30	11 45	12 30	1 55	2 45	2 45	2 50	3 30	3 45
Dymchurch ...	dep.	10 48	12 03	12 48	2 13	Z	3 03	3 08	3 40	4 03
St. Mary's Bay ...	dep.	10 53	12 08	12 53	2 18	The Bluecoaster Limited	3 08	3 13	3 53	4 08
New Romney { arr.		11 05	12 20	1 05	2 30		3 20	3 25	4 05	4 20
New Romney { dep.		11 10	12*25	1 10	2 35		3 25	—	—	4 25
Greatstone ...	dep.	11 15	12*30	1 15	2A40		—	—	—	—
Maddieson's Camp	dep.	11 20	12*35	1 20	2A45		—	—	—	—
Dungeness ...	arr.	11 40	—	1 40	2†55	3 30	3 45	—	—	4 50

DOWN

		B	A	B	A	A	B	A		
		p.m.	p.m.	p.m.	p.m.	p.m.	p.m.	p.m.		p.m
Hythe	dep.	4 30	4 45	5 35	5 45	6 15	6 30	7 00	—	7 30
Dymchurch ...	dep.	4 48	5 03	5 53	6 03	6 33	6 48	7 18	—	7 43
St. Mary's Bay ...	dep.	4 53	5 08	5 58	6 08	6 38	6 53	7 23	—	7 53
New Romney { arr.		5 05	5 20	6 10	6 20	6 50	7 05	7 35	—	8 05
New Romney { dep.		5 10	5 25	6*15	6*25	—	7*10	—		8*10
Greatstone ...	dep.	5 15	5 30	6*20	6*30	—	7*15	—		8*15
Maddieson's Camp	dep.	5 20	5 35	6*25	6*35	—	7*20	—		8*20
Dungeness ...	arr.	5 35	5 55	—	—	—	—	—		—

NOTES—A—30th June 21st September only.

B—May 19th June 29th and 22nd September 2nd October only.

*—Only travels beyond New Romney if required.

Z—Seats bookable in advance on The Bluecoaster Limited

†—Arrives 3.05 p.m. 30th June, 1949-21st September, 1949.

Tuesdays, an interesting reflection of a side of the railway's operations that does not appear in the published timetables.

The omission of Tuesdays is because the path is needed for a holiday camp special. The railway has run these for some years, a typical week's schedules being as shown (in the table). The trains are not charters, revenue being dependent on the number of passengers using them, and there is a tendency to cut down their numbers.

Typical Weekly Schedule of Special Trains during Pre-Consortium Years. 1971 Peak Season

NB Most workings involve some ECS running but this is not shown in detail.

MONDAY
12.30   New Romney–Maddieson's Camp. Loco each end. Takes campers back from ramble. Return ECS.
 1.45   Golden Sands–Hythe. Shoppers special. Returns as 2.25 shuttle.
 5.20   Hythe–Golden Sands. ECS to New Romney.

TUESDAY
12.35   New Romney–Golden Sands. Only if required (party too large for service train). Return ECS.
 1.30   Maddieson's Camp–Hythe. Shoppers special. Return as 2.25 shuttle.
 5.20   Hythe–Maddieson's Camp. Shoppers special. Return ECS to New Romney.

WEDNESDAY
 2.10   Golden Sands–Maddieson's Camp. Strengthened service train.
 5.00   Maddieson's Camp–Golden Sands. Strengthened service trains.

THURSDAY
 1.45   Maddieson's Camp–Dungeness.
 3.00   Dungeness–Maddieson's Camp–New Romney. (Party from Maddieson's Camber Camp plus Littlestone campers.)
 4.25   New Romney–Dungeness (Camber party).

ROMNEY, HYTHE & DYMCHURCH LIGHT RAILWAY

Date 11th July 1973

TRAIN REGISTER

Station: NEW ROMNEY

Hythe — H
Dymchurch — D
St. Mary's Bay — B
New Romney — R
Dungeness — Ds

UP TRAINS

Train No.	Destination	Line Clear Asked	Line Clear Given	Section Received Entering Train	Section Sent Out of Train	Line Clear Asked	Line Clear Received	Train Entering Section Sent	Train Out of Section Received	Arrival	Departure
5	H	SERVICE				920	920	925	937 Ds	-915	-915
10	H	SERVICE				931	931	1025	1034	-1025	-1025
9	H	SERVICE				1034	1034	1115	1124 Ds	-1115	-1115
5	H	1140 Ex Ds				1124	1124	1215	1220	-1212 1215	-1212 1215
2	H	SERVICE				1224	1224	1·15	123	-1·15	-1·15
10	H	SERVICE				123	123	153	200 Ds	-153	-153
9	H	1335 Ex Ds				200	200	216	225	-205 216	-206
2	H	SERVICE				225	225	306	314 Ds	-306	-306
5	H	1445 Ex Ds				314	314	339	348	-334 339	-334 339
1	H	SIGNAL				348	348	351	400	-351	-351
9	H	SERVICE				400	400	415	424 Ds	-415	-415
10	H	1620 Ex Ds				424	424	457	509	-452 505	-452 505
2	H	1735 Ex Ds				509	509	510	619	-603 610	-603 610
						619	619				

DOWN TRAINS

Train No.	Destination	Line Clear Asked	Line Clear Given	Section Received Entering Train	Section Sent Out of Train	Arrival	Departure	Line Clear Received	Train Entering Section Sent	Train Out of Section Received
9	R		920	1011	1021		Stop	P.WAY DEPT		—
5	Ds		1027	1048	1057		110	TABLET.		—
10	R		1057	1147	1157		Stop	SERVICE		—
9	Ds		1157	1244	1254	1254	1256	TABLET.		—
5	Ds		1255	201	208		212	TABLET.		—
2	R		208	237	207		Stop	SERVICE		—
10	Ds		247	317	327		333	TABLET.		—
9	R		321	350	400		Stop	SERVICE		—
2	Ds		400	403	450		457	TABLET.		—
5	R		460	454	503		Stop	ECS 6¼ MILE		—
1	R		503	511	520		Stop	SERVICE		—
9	R		520	548	551		Stop	SERVICE		—
10	R		557	619	631		Stop	SERVICE		—
2			631							

(signature) 11/7/73

A typical daily train register page for New Romney Station

L

2.15   Maddieson's Camp–Golden Sands. Strengthened service train.
5.10   Golden Sands–Maddieson's Camp. Strengthened service train.

FRIDAY
3.15   Dungeness–New   Romney.   Strengthened   service   train
Maddieson's party from St Margaret's Bay).

The intensive service, and timetable complications, require that the administration of the line is careful and accurate. Services are controlled by a traffic manager working through stationmasters at the main stations and the associated complications of the locomotive rostering are overseen by an operating manager who ensures as even a balance as possible in the allocation of drivers' turns. If one considers that the engineman, besides driving, firing and generally seeing to his locomotive, is also in control of his train's safety, that the longest 'turn' involves 77 miles or approximately the same as three times round the railway in a period of $8\frac{1}{2}$ hours, and that the engineman must in addition carry out routine servicing both before and after his shift it will be realised that strict fairness is needed. Train operating jobs on the railway are no sinecure and neither are those of the signalmen and station staff. The railway is run with block signalling on the double track and a token on the Dungeness line. The block sections are Hythe–Dymchurch; Dymchurch–St Mary's Bay; St Mary's Bay–New Romney; New Romney–Dungeness. Train control is by telephonic communication, St Mary's Bay being 'switched out' if not needed, and a detailed train register (example on page 177) is kept at each block station. Major road crossings are flagged.

Communication between the stations is currently by private GPO telephone line on the New Romney–Hythe section and by the public telephone on the Dungeness section. There is evidence—mainly in the shape of surviving poles—that the railway originally had its own internal telephone system but this has certainly not been in existence since the war.

A Note on the Finances

The finances of the Romney Hythe & Dymchurch Light Railway Company always depended very heavily on one man, Captain J. E. P. Howey. The original share capital, of which the Captain held some 99 per cent, was £34,000 with powers to borrow up to £8,000 more if needed. Henry Greenly made great play at the public inquiry with figures showing that the declared capital was adequate but in fact it was not nearly sufficient for the ever-increasing visions of the promoter. Capital was increased to £51,000 for the Dungeness extension, increased yet further by borrowing to a total of £68,000 and this has ever since remained the railway's declared capital cost, with minor modifications. In reality the completed railway cost almost twice as much, a total of £117,003 broken down as shown below. The Captain regularised the position in 1932 by making a gift to the railway of £61,680 which was shown as a writing down of the value of all assets. The book values of railway assets have since remained fairly constant, although Red Tiles was sold to the Captain in 1938 at a written-down value of £2,036 and the twelve railway cottages were also sold to him in 1946 at a similar total sum.

	1929 cost/value	1933 value
Permanent way & works	£52,511	£23,549
Buildings and land	£28,058	£13,529
Locomotives	£13,941	£ 7,038
Rolling stock	£22,435	£10,718
Plant & equipment	£ 1,058	£ 529

Further equipment such as the CPRs and the 1934–5 saloons were apparently financed out of revenue and not assimilated into capital book stock. The railway has always been restricted by the amount of capital authorised by its light railway order and by the restriction on borrowing to a total of not more than one third of the authorised capital. Indeed a new LRO has been applied for mainly to remove this restriction.

The paper profits and losses of the revenue account are shown below. It should be remembered that these are not operating surpluses or deficits but what remains after all maintenance, stock, etc requirements have been met.

1928–9	LOSS	£6,099	1951	LOSS	£ 209
1930	,,	£2,957	1952	,,	£1,121
1931	PROFIT	£ 23	1953	PROFIT	£2,038
1932	,,	£ 680	1954	,,	£2,059
1933	,,	£1,569	1955	,,	£2,662
1934	,,	£ 791	1956	,,	£1,232
1935	LOSS	£ 836	1957	,,	£4,755
1936	,,	£2,756	1958	,,	£3,013
1937	,,	£ 737	1959	,,	£3,997
1938	,,	£1,410	1960	,,	£1,933
1939	,,	£ 336	1961	,,	£2,547
1940	,,	£ 52	1962	,,	£3,563
1941	PROFIT	£ 805	1963	,,	£1,677
1942	,,	£ 453	1964	,,	£1,782
1943	,,	£ 579	1965	,,	£3,036
1944	,,	£ 529	1966	,,	£3,703
1945	,,	£ 231	1967	,,	£3,650
1946	,,	£4,042	1968	,,	£2,516
1947	,,	£2,433	1969	,,	£5,034
1948	,,	£4,168	1970	,,	£3,011
1949	,,	£3,764	1971	,,	£3,793
1950	,,	£ 485	1972	,,	£2,848

All profit figures are before tax. Note that dividends have been paid only from 1966–70 inclusive and that the railway cannot be said ever to have been really profitable in view of the capital invested.

A Note on the Tickets

The RH & D has always used Edmundson card tickets for the majority of its ticket issues, buying the first from Williamson & Co of Ashton under Lyme and latterly (since 1972) from British Rail's ticket printing works at Crewe. Typical samples are shown on page 182 and there is not a great deal to be said about them.

Originally the tickets covered nearly all permutations of possible journeys and this was perpetuated in the early post-war ordering—with the result that the railway still holds massive stocks of such mildly esoteric issues as St Mary's Bay to Greatstone (single). Initially there was a logical system of colour-coding by destination station but this broke down after the war and an attempt is only now being made to colour code by ticket type. An interesting point is that up to 1972 there were no children's tickets. Single journeys were covered by cutting an adult single ticket in half diagonally and charging half fare. For a return journey an adult single, overstamped child return, was used with the accounting anomaly that a child's return journey cost two-thirds of the appropriate adult fare instead of half. Excursion tickets have also been issued at various times and are clearly marked as such.

On the Dungeness route, tickets from intermediate stations are issued by a travelling guard who also issues Dungeness tickets when the booking office there is not open. These tickets are of bus-type from a ticket machine.

Parties have long been catered for by the issue of standard-pattern paper vouchers detailing the number of travellers, etc, and with counterfoils that are retained for accounting purposes. For some holiday camp parties these are replaced by individual cinema-pattern tickets which are issued to each member of the party. The various holiday camps also hold their own stocks of tickets to cover certain

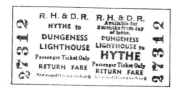

Specimen tickets of the railway, mostly of the immediate post-war period

popular journeys on an excursion basis. The camps concerned are:
School Journeys Centre, St Mary's Bay: to Hythe, New Romney,
Dungeness; Golden Sands: to Maddieson's Camp; Beach Holiday
Camp: to Hythe; Maddieson's: to Hythe, Golden Sands (Maddieson's
own Golden Sands and there is a regular interchange of campers
for sporting events, etc).

There are also pram, bicycle and dog tickets which see fairly
regular use and there are in existence platform tickets for all the
main stations. These are not generally in use and indeed, in the case
of Dungeness, for example, it would be very difficult to enforce them.

It may be of interest to note the number (in round thousands) and
proportions of tickets issued by the main stations in a typical year.
The overall figures for 1972 are shown below.

Ordinary tickets:	Place	Number
	Hythe	53,000
	Dymchurch	24,000
	St Mary's Bay	6,000
	New Romney	31,000
	Dungeness	5,000
	Travelling Guard	15,000
	Paper vouchers	3–4,000 (17,000 people)
	Holiday Camps	
	—School Journeys Centre	20,000
	—Others	6,000

These produced a total of some 302,000 passenger journeys.

Notes on the Visits of RH & DR Locomotives to Ravenglass: 1925 and 1971

1925: 'GREEN GODDESS'

'The Trials of Captain Howey's new 15in gauge Pacific Locomotive on the R & E Railway.

A ten days track trial of Mr Henry Greenly's latest 15in gauge locomotive, one of the two ordered from Messrs Davey Paxman and Co Ltd, for Captain J. E. P. Howey and the late Count Zborowski, have just been completed at Eskdale by kind permission of Sir Aubrey Brocklebank, Bart.

The new engine has proved eminently satisfactory to both owner, builders and designer, and while the Eskdale Railway is not altogether suited to speed trials, 35 miles an hour was obtained for about half a mile without any extreme effort on the part of the locomotive and its driver. The hoped-for top speed of 40 miles per hour therefore seems easily possible.

Although the engine has a nominal tractive effort of only two-thirds of that of the *Esk* locomotive, the test load of 34 tons showed that the careful attention to balance and valve gear design allowed the horsepower of the boiler to be fully utilised. The best load negotiated by the *Esk* during her trials was 29 tons (but this was with the unsatisfactory Lentz poppet valves—author). With 20 coaches—a 160 passenger train—a speed of $22\frac{1}{2}$ miles an hour average was attained between Irton Road and Walkmill, this including acceleration and deceleration at each end of the timed run.

Further particulars of the design will be published in due course. For the moment it may be stated that no failure in any part of the general design was observed, the final portion of the trials being required more or less to decide which was the better brake—the simple vacuum or the straight-line Westinghouse.

184

The Walschaerts gear proved itself in every respect. It was possible to run light in mid-gear, while heavy fast trains could be hauled with the valve gear linked up to 35 per cent cut off.

The Cartazzi controls of the trailing radial axle worked very well and there was no doubt at all about the efficiency of the piston valves. The chief day of the trials was Sunday, June 29, and among the visitors were Capt R. B. Howey, Capt R. Clive Gallon, Capt R. P. Spencer, Major H. Simpson of Carlisle, Mr A. J. Greenly, Mr J. A. Holder, Mr Terence Holder and of course Capt J. E. Howey and H. Greenly. Mr R. Hardie, the outdoor superintendent of the R & E line, worked most assiduously in providing everything necessary to the success of the tests and thanks are due to Mr Gillon, the Manager, for his assistance. The name of the new engine is the *Green Goddess*.

Getting the engine unloaded from the main line was not the least interesting feature of the visit. This feat was accomplished in two hours and twenty minutes and a run was made the same afternoon.

On bench tests 40ihp had been obtained. No nosing or rolling was experienced at any speed up to the maximum obtained, and no 'period' in the balance was experienced. As Capt Gallon remarked, at 35 miles per hour the engine appeared to "go to sleep".

The *Green Goddess* is a 24ft 9in long, weighs 7 tons 15cwts in running order and just over 6 tons empty. The adhesive weight is 6,600lb and the tractive effort at 160lb pressure is 1,470lb.'

—*Model Engineer and Light Machinery Review*: 30 July 1925

1971: 'NORTHERN CHIEF'

'*Northern Chief* on the R & ER.

Northern Chief was at Ravenglass from Friday October 29th, to Monday, 15 November. Driver Terry Whawell of the RH & DR was in charge of her throughout the trial.

Northern Chief was unloaded at lunch time, was steamed immediately and made its first run to Dalegarth with a light train in the late afternoon, arriving back at Ravenglass after dark, travelling down from Dalegarth tender first.

The following morning it was found that, although the wheelbase of the engine was exactly the same as the length of the turntable it was possible to turn the engine by barring it backwards and forwards to clear the rail ends. The engine was thus able to be turned at each end of the line after this.

During a preliminary trial on Sunday the 31st, *Northern Chief*'s tender became derailed near Spout House when a pair of wheels dropped between the rails due to a wheel being loose on the axle. After this fault was rectified on the Monday, and the track in the area had been resleepered, the engine was again steamed and a train coupled on comprising 9×20 seater open coaches and 6×20 seater saloons, weight approximately 18 tons. This train, being empty of passengers, was reckoned to be approaching the same weight as a fully loaded 9 coach train, taking into consideration the friction on curves, etc, due to the extra length of 15 coaches. On a dry rail *Northern Chief* managed this load quite well and was able to keep to our timings without much trouble and without any slipping of the driving wheels. However, *Northern Chief* has no sanding gear at all and, later in the week, when the rain came, it was a rather different story.

On these trips *Northern Chief* was burning coal obtained locally which was very dirty stuff and which put up quite a remarkable smoke screen over the length of Eskdale.

On the following days coke was used as fuel and the engine steamed very well on it. However, some trouble was experienced with the fusible plug in the firebox (a slight leak developing round the screw thread) and Terry Whawell decided to go back onto coal in case the coke was having some effect on the plug. The nett result was some very black looking passengers in the front open coaches on the return journeys from Dalegarth when the engine was not pulling hard.

On the five days when the engine ran as advertised for the general public the weather was very poor, being cold and damp. The train was shortened to six coaches as *Northern Chief* was slipping badly due to having no sanding gear and the fact that the driver was unfamiliar with the track.

On Sunday, 7 November, *River Esk* and *Northern Chief* double-headed a train to Dalegarth and back. The two engines which were both designed by Henry Greenly and built by Davey Paxman at Colchester had never previously been within 250 miles of one another —an historic occasion. Unfortunately the weather was foul and few good pictures of the event resulted.

During the rest of the fortnight that the *Northern Chief* was on the line, runs were made with varying loads in all sorts of conditions.

The opportunity was taken to let all the RH & ER drivers take a turn at handling the engine so that as many different impressions could be obtained as possible.

Northern Chief is of course a completely different type of loco from *River Esk* and was designed to do completely different work. The principal statistics show this clearly:

	River Esk saturated	Northern Chief superheated
Cylinders	$6'' \times 8\frac{1}{2}''$	$5\frac{1}{4}'' \times 8\frac{1}{2}''$
Driving Wheels	8 coupled	6 coupled
Diameter	$17\frac{1}{2}''$	$25\frac{1}{2}''$
Tractive effort (nominal)	2,400lb	1,400lb

As would be expected, the larger driving wheel on *Northern Chief* gave the engine an extremely smooth gait in contrast to *River Esk*'s fussy motion at speed. We were not, however, prepared for the astonishingly smooth ride of *Northern Chief*. Nor perhaps did we expect him to hold his feet so well, considering the lack of sanding gear, nor to to handle the trains with such apparent ease.

CONCLUSIONS

The object in bringing *Northern Chief* to Ravenglass was to see how much we could learn from the performance of a Romney engine on our line, bearing in mind our intention to design and build a new loco *Sir Arthur Heywood* at Ravenglass.

Northern Chief had, considering the nominal tractive effort, remarkable power. However, while it handled the test trains comfortably on the move, it needed everything it possessed to get the train away again on even a moderate gradient.

The fact that it had only six driving wheels did not affect its ability to keep its feet; in fact there seemed to be even less tendency to slip than with our eight coupled engines.

The larger driving wheels are not a disadvantage either, so far as slipping goes. However, more power will be needed from our new engine and the wheels would not have to be as large as *Northern Chief*'s.

The ride was incredibly smooth. This can be put down to the semi-elliptic rubber-mounted springs, the four wheel bogie leading and the well balanced engine. With a six-coupled layout it is easier to bring the centre of gravity forward so that the weight of the boiler is more over the centre driven axle and so that there is sufficient weight on the leading wheels.

Superheating is a subject which has caused much discussion over the years. We are still not convinced that the advantages are so great as to make it worth our while adopting it on the R & ER. Due to the smaller number of boiler tubes, *Northern Chief* took appreciably longer to raise steam in the morning. On the other hand, the pressure was held steady with less trouble during a run. It was noticeable that the super-heater only made much difference when the engine was pulling fairly fast. Undoubtedly, saving in water and fuel could be made on the run to Dalegarth but there would be little advantage on the return journey when the grades are mostly with the train. It is also debateable whether the superheater on *Northern Chief* worked as well when coke was being burnt.

On the whole we consider that simplicity, and so easier maintenance, must be the most vital feature of our engines. This is far more important than the saving of fuel.

Other features we noted were the pilot valve on the regulator and automatic relief valves on the cylinders, both of which we may well adopt. We noted also that the rigid six-coupled wheel-base of *Northern Chief* did not take kindly to our more severe curves showing the need for flexibility here even with six drivers.

One interesting fact which emerged, about which we were a little concerned, was the smooth riding of our new coaches at speeds far higher than those at which we normally run.

Northern Chief really got into his stride on some occasions, particularly between Black Bridge and Walk Mill, but the short wheelbase bogies did not hunt at this speed as we had feared.'

R & ER Co report in Newsletter No 44.

Future Plans

The new owners of the RH & DR realise full well that the railway has been living on borrowed time for well over a decade now. Consequently a great deal of change will occur over the next few years. It is not possible at this stage to predict with complete accuracy what will happen but the long term plans are as summarised below; they are likely to be adhered to at least in broad outline.

Stations, tracks and fittings
The current state of the track is not entirely satisfactory. It is still laid mainly with ex-World War I surplus rail. The majority of this is American flat-bottomed rail of 25lb/yd which, while well worn, probably has another 25 to 40 years life if re-used selectively. Apart from about three quarters of a mile of ex-Sierra Leone 30lb/yd rail, the remainder in 1973 was original Belgian 12kg/metre material which is susceptible to web corrosion and which will need replacing probably within the next 10 to 15 years or so. About one and a half miles of Sierra Leone rail are stockpiled to meet this need.

The rail situation is therefore reasonable but the track suffers from two major defects. It is laid largely on ex-BR sleepers of indifferent quality with poor fastenings and is very susceptible to track creep. This has led over the years to buckling and to large numbers of open joints which have been filled with very short rail lengths. It is therefore proposed to relay complete sections using long lengths of rail at the rate of about two miles per year. Experiments are being made with Jarrah sleepers, steel sleepers and concrete ones to see which will give the best results.

Major rebuildings are planned at Hythe and New Romney stations both to improve the railway's public image and to increase covered storage space. The proposed layouts are shown diagramatically on page 203. Briefly:

(i) At Hythe, the present overall roof will be retained but the station buildings are being scrapped and replaced by a proper roofed concourse area with a shop and booking facilities; toilets will be built by the local council but on railway land. The tracks by No four platform will be removed and replaced by an access road to a new car park on the present allotments; the other platforms will be extended towards the signal box with appropriate track modifications and access to the turntable will be solely from the existing spur off the down main line. The shed will probably be used as a carriage workshop for some years. Partial completion is envisaged for 1974, with the layout alterations following afterwards.

(ii) At New Romney a fairly drastic alteration is transforming the main station into a more operationally convenient state. The up-side will be remodelled to give a terminal loop and siding, the 'office road' will be lowered and made into a loop and a large overall roof will span five of the tracks to provide covered carriage storage space in the winter. The timescale at present envisaged would bring these alterations into full use for the 1974 season.

(iii) For operational purposes a new passing loop is required on the Dungeness line. This will be at Maddieson's Camp and will be arranged as shown on page 203. It will have home and starter colour light signals and a road bridge will replace the present level-crossing at the camp entrance.

Locomotives

Future timetables envisage a six-engine service and it is expected that the whole stud will be overhauled with the idea of having all nine available simultaneously from about 1976. It is at present intended to have one or two locomotives overhauled by outside contractors each year and this is likely to be done by Cushing's of Rainham since they have made a superb job of the machines renewed so far (*Dr Syn* and *Hurricane*). If the experiments with oil firing on *Winston Churchill* are successful, other engines will be so equipped. The purchase of a main line diesel is not very likely since its anticipated use would not be sufficient properly to amortise the capital required, (ie in total terms it would probably be more expensive to operate than a single-manned oil-fired steam locomotive). Lastly *The Bug*, although the private property of Mr McAlpine, is likely to be restored and kept on the railway.

Coaches

This is probably the most urgent need and a considerable programme of coach rebuilding is being undertaken. Present plans over the next few years envisage:

Up to 30   20-seater standard saloons
about 15   16-seater opens rebuilt to the new style
     5   6-seat/luggage brakes on 8XX series chassis/Clayton chassis
     1   16-seater saloon on 8XX series chassis
     1   Platelayers tool van
  5–6   12-seater first class coaches on the former Clayton chassis, probably with heating and lighting for winter service.

It should be possible by this means and by conserving some of the best of the existing stock both to raise the standards and to lower the number of coaches in use. It is envisaged that in the longer term a few non-standard coaches including the Heywoods may be restored for future special use. Present intention, so far as livery is concerned, is to varnish new stock, paint improved stock in brown and cream and leave the short-life stock in green and cream. The new railway crest will be affixed to all new and modified stock.

Train services

Plans for these are more tenuous but timetables are likely to be gradually improved to give more frequent trains—especially to Dungeness—and the operating season is likely to be extended. Winter weekend working is a distinct possibility, at least between New Romney and Hythe.

INDEX TO PLANS

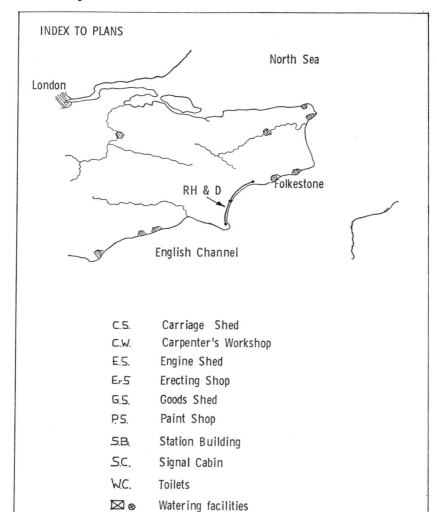

C.S.	Carriage Shed
C.W.	Carpenter's Workshop
E.S.	Engine Shed
E.r.S	Erecting Shop
G.S.	Goods Shed
P.S.	Paint Shop
S.B.	Station Building
S.C.	Signal Cabin
W.C.	Toilets
⊠ ⊗	Watering facilities
⊤⊤⊤	Platform
—+—	Standard Gauge
——	Narrow Gauge
- - -	Lifted Railways
—·—	Railway Boundaries

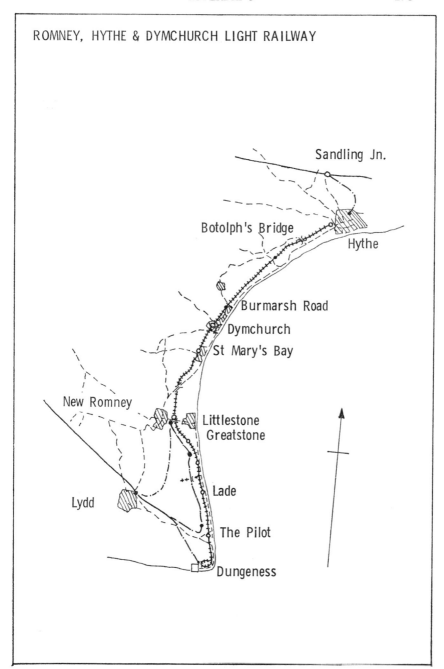

ROMNEY, HYTHE & DYMCHURCH LIGHT RAILWAY

Sandling Jn.

Botolph's Bridge

Hythe

Burmarsh Road

Dymchurch

St Mary's Bay

New Romney

Littlestone
Greatstone

Lade

Lydd

The Pilot

Dungeness

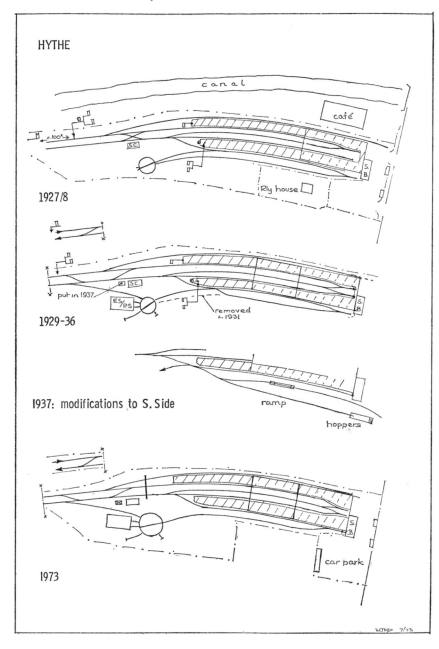

HYTHE

1927/8

1929-36

1937: modifications to S. Side

1973

DYMCHURCH

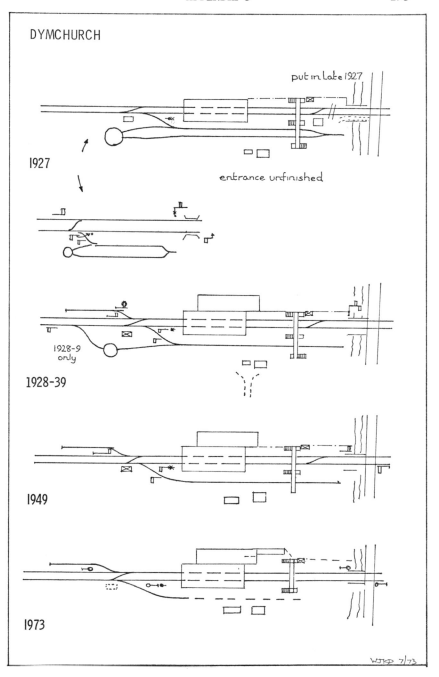

put in Late 1927

1927

entrance unfinished

1928-39

1928-9
only

1949

1973

WJKD 7/73

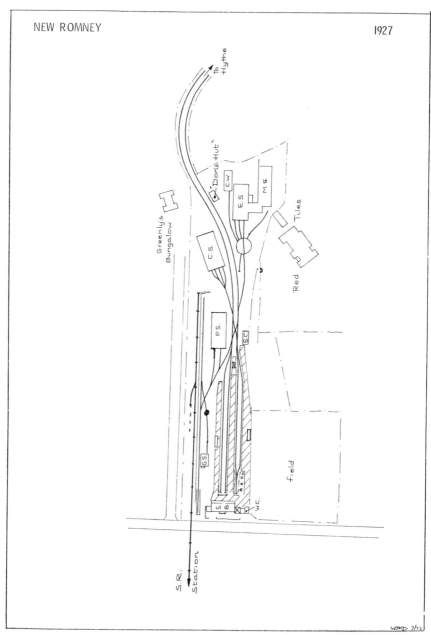

NEW ROMNEY   1927

NEW ROMNEY

1928/9

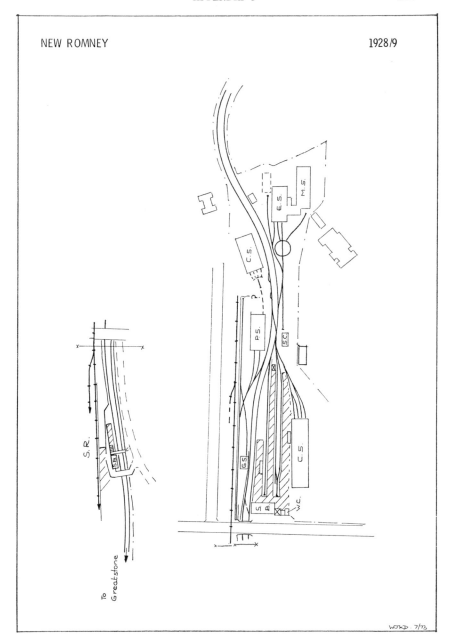

WORD. 7/73

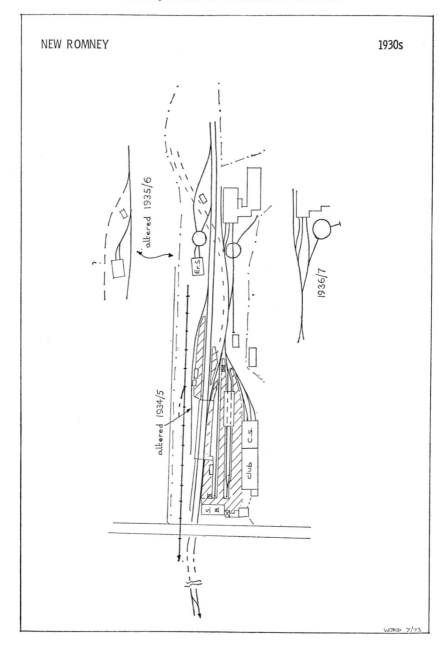

NEW ROMNEY

1930s

WJRD 7/73

NEW ROMNEY　　　　　　　　　　　　　　1972/3

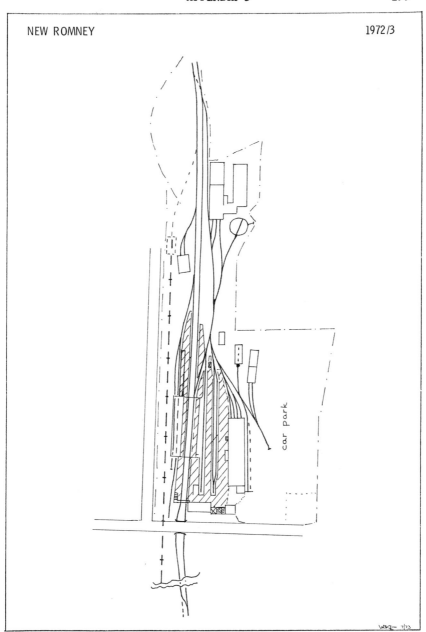

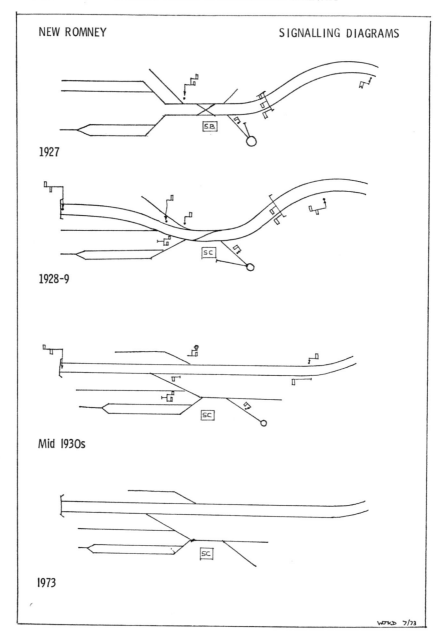

NEW ROMNEY

SIGNALLING DIAGRAMS

1927

1928-9

Mid 1930s

1973

WTKD 7/73

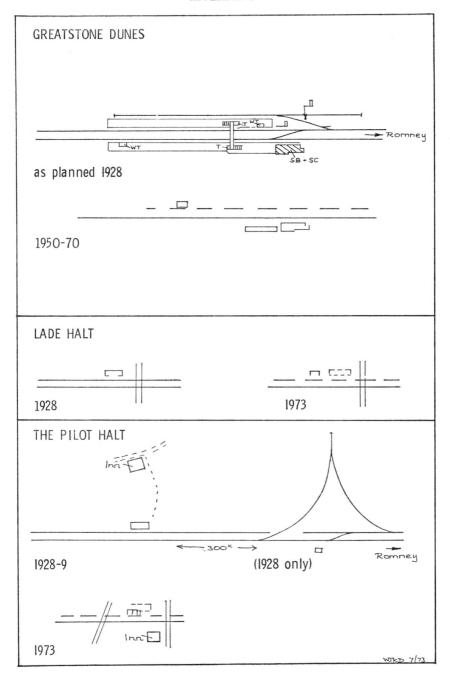

GREATSTONE DUNES

as planned 1928

Romney

SB + SC

1950-70

LADE HALT

1928   1973

THE PILOT HALT

Inn

1928-9   (1928 only)   Romney

←— 300ˣ —→

1973

Inn

WJKD 7/73

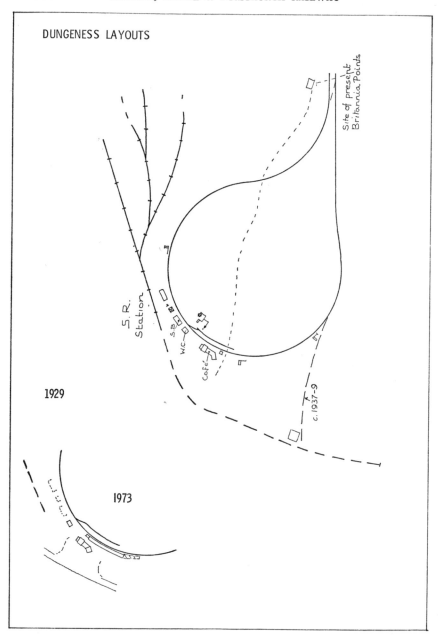

DUNGENESS LAYOUTS

1929

1973

PROPOSED LAYOUT ALTERATIONS   as at August 1973

Hythe

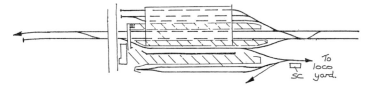

NEW ROMNEY

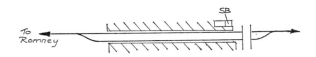

Maddieson's Camp

NB Signalling arrangements not finalised

WJT-D 8/73

Bibliography

As with the R & ER, there is very little definitive published material on the RH & DR and most of the material in this book has been gathered from private recollections, newspaper files and magazine articles. The main sources of printed information are given below but some conflict of detail is apparent.

Minimum Gauge Railways (Sir A. P. Heywood) 3rd Edn 1896
ABC of Narrow Gauge Railways (W. J. K. Davies) 1961
Miniature Railways (R. Butterell) 1964
Miniature Steam Locomotives (G. Woodcock) 1964
The World's Smallest Railway (Dr P. Ransome-Wallis) Successive editions
The Line that Jack Built 1968
Miniature Railways Vol 1: 15in Gauge (Butterell/et al) 1972
The Duffield Bank and Eaton Railways (H. Clayton) 1968
The Romney Hythe and Dymchurch Railway (R. Kidner) 1967
The Miniature World of Henry Greenly (E. A. and E. H. Steel) 1973
The following periodicals were consulted: *The Marshlander; Models, Railways and Locomotives; The Locomotive; Model Engineer; Railway Magazine; Railway World.*

Author's Notes and Acknowledgements

Five years ago I wrote of the satisfaction of being able to compile the history of a British minor railway that was still doing its original job (the Ravenglass & Eskdale). It is even more satisfying to have been able to complete the double by being invited to write the history of the other major 15in gauge line in this country. The Romney, Hythe & Dymchurch Light Railway, after some anxious moments in recent years, is also flourishing and is indeed still carrying out the task it was originally built to undertake. If it is much younger than its northern counterpart, it is none-the-less just as fascinating, for it must be one of the few railways to have been created almost wholly by one man. Henry Greenly not only designed the original locomotives and stock, he also laid out the route, undertook the preliminary negotiations, supervised the construction and was responsible for the 1,001 fittings that go to make up a railway, from buildings to point indicators. If some of his work has not stood the test of time, much of it has and I hope this book will be at least something of a tribute to Greenly and to the line's promoter and owner Captain J. E. P. Howey.

One problem of this integrity of design is that the history of the 'Romney' is, much more than usual, really a series of histories. The track, buildings, locomotives, rolling stock, all have their own clear lines of development along with the operational side and the human history. To keep these clear I have felt it desirable to follow each of the major aspects separately, even at the cost of some repetition of facts. Thus the main 'history' in chapters one to seven does not go deeply into technical detail unless it affects specifically the overall story. The technical histories are incorporated in the following three chapters.

In spite of the railway's youth, the research for this volume has, like that for the R & ER, been extremely frustrating for very few records of the early days survive. The book is again very definitely a co-operative venture. In particular Messrs G. A. Barlow, A. A. Binfield and N. E. Danger have all in their separate ways made the final manuscript possible and without their help and criticism there would be no book. The railway company has always been very helpful, allowing me the freedom of its line, providing facilities for research—and producing what records do still exist! Many others have helped: Col D. I. L. Beath, H. Bowtell, A. Crowhurst, A. Ganfield, Major J. T. Holder, S. Leleux, P. C. Hawkins, J. Morley, J. B. Snell, T. Whawell, J. Wootton, and A. Wells have searched their memories and provided useful information; the RH & D Association's journal *The Marshlander* has been a constant source of assistance; the local papers, in particular the *Folkstone Herald,* provided plenty of facts—and fancies—about the periods when the railway was in the public eye. To George Barlow and Terry Whawell I owe a special debt of gratitude for the privilege of travelling on *Northern Chief* over R & ER metals. If I have forgotten anyone, I apologise.

The photographs in this book come from:
(i) Collection of the late Captain J. E. P. Howey (Courtesy RH & DR)
(ii) Collection of G. A. Barlow
(iii) Locomotive and General Railway Photographs
(iv) The author's collection
(v) A. Crowhurst

Lastly I must especially thank Mr and Mrs E. A. Steel for information on Henry Greenly.

Index

NOTE: Because of the nature of the line's history, most information on specific aspects is grouped together. Index entries therefore make only broad references (eg Locomotives, rather than noting each individual one; they are all summed up in a few related pages).